THE RED ARMY TOWARDS THE ODER
THEN AND NOW

Edited by Daniel Taylor

An Imprint of Pen & Sword Books Ltd

The Red Army Towards the Oder – Then and Now
© After the Battle and Daniel Taylor, 2023

Published by After the Battle
An imprint of Pen & Sword Books Ltd
47 Church Street, Barnsley,
South Yorkshire, S70 2AS
Tel. 01226 734222
Fax. 01226 734438
Email: enquiries@pen-and-sword.co.uk
Website: **www.afterthebattle.com**
            www.pen-and-sword.co.uk

Printed and bound in India by Replika Press Pvt. Ltd.

ISBN: 978 1 399059 03 9

Commissioning Editor: Rob Green
Editor: Daniel Taylor
Design: Paul Wilkinson
Cover Design: Jon Wilkinson

Credits:
This book is based on the following published articles which appeared in *After the Battle* magazine:
'The Oder Bridgeheads, 1945' by Tomasz Zgoda (Issue 184, May 2019).
'The Battle for Festung Posen, 1945' by Tomasz Zgoda (Issue 188, August 2020).
'The Battle for Festung Küstrin' by Tomasz Zgoda (Issue 192, August 2021).

Acknowledgements:
We are indebted to Tomasz Zgoda for his phenomenal work in compiling the history of this crucial, though frequently overlooked, portion of World War II history. Rob Green, the commissioning editor has provided enthusiastic support and guidance to ensure that the material required was in place. As ever, Paul Wilkinson and his brother Jon have contributed their usual deft design skills to the layout and cover design. Though rarely noted, the involvement of a number of proof readers is essential in ensuring that the completed work is accessible to a wide range of readers, with differing levels of military familiarity. In this role I would like to highlight the assistance of Peter Rhodes, Angus Taylor, Joseph Taylor and Penny Malik whose contribution cannot be overplayed.

Front Cover
Above: An SU-152 assault gun disabled and abandoned on what was Kurfürsten-Ring in Posen in February 1945. Below: The Polish name for this road in Poznan was Waly Zygmunta Starego, though post-war it became Niepodleglosci (Independence) Avenue. Building No. 8 has been splendidly restored and today houses an office of the Polish railway service.

Rear Cover
Top left: A Russian howitzer being used to clear city blocks in desperate street fighting in what was then Breite Strasse, Posen. *Top right:* The comparison was found at the junction of Wielka Street and Kydowska.

Middle left: A Sherman M4A2, supplied to the Soviet Army by the United States under Lend/Lease, lies knocked-out under a railway underpass in Küstrin. *Bottom right*: Today the graffitied viaduct carries the Szczecin to Wroclaw railway line, showing no sign of the historic events that unfolded on this spot. The city became Kostrzyn nad Odra after the war.

Bottom: An original colour image of the Niederwutzen cellulose factory in Zehden. The proximity of Germany's capital is abundantly clear.

CONTENTS

INTRODUCTION 6
THE SOVIET DASH TO THE ODER 8

PART 1: FESTUNG POSEN
German Siege Preparations 10
Alarm 17
Red Army at the Gates 22nd to 25th January 19
Soviet Substitution 21
The Southern and Western Districts 26th January to 3rd February 21
The Northern Districts 26th January to 16th February 29
The Eastern Districts 21st January to 17th February 32
Fighting for the Old Town 18th to 23rd February 42
Storming the Citadel 51
The Cost 65

PART II: DEFENDING THE ODER
THE SCHWEDT BRIDGEHEAD
Skorzeny 66
German Defences 72
The Red Army's Arrival 75
Counter-Attack 78
Sonnernwende 84
Withdrawal 87
THE ZEHDEN BRIDGEHEAD
Buildup 96
The Gathering Storm 100
One Last Push 106

PART III: FESTUNG KÜSTRIN
Last Days Before The Siege 112
First Contact 117
Stalemate 125
Fall of the Neustadt 126
Envelopment 135
Endgame 140
Die Arbrechnung 147

THE BEGINNING OF THE END 149

ORGANISATION TABLES 150
GLOSSARY 152

INTRODUCTION

THIS WORK HAS BEEN BASED on three articles written for *After the Battle* magazine by the Polish author Tomasz Zgoda. Born in Poland and living in Poznan, Tomasz is intimately familiar with the locations fought over in early 1945 and has explored the former battlefield extensively. His familiarity with the Polish, German and Russian languages has allowed him to consult documents and accounts from all three perspectives, offering insights rarely seen in most western accounts of the fighting on the Eastern Front. In particular his access to the original war diaries of Russian formations

provides the narrative of the military operations with an unparalleled level of detail.

Editing the work of another writer is a heavy responsibility. In this respect I hope I have achieved more of a sympathetic translation than a refinement of the text. The primary goal when adapting the text was that, in melding the three works together, the result retains the truth of the original, whilst ensuring that it flows together as single, comprehensible and readable narrative. Escaping the tight limitations of the magazine format and given the freedom afforded by a book, there has been space to expand on the original and enhance the presentation of the images.

One key area where the presentation has been changed is in the names used to explain locations. As originally presented, the text led with the Polish names but the maps provided were chiefly of wartime, German provenance. The ability to quickly orientate the reader was judged paramount and so the text now leads with the German name to conform to the mapping whilst showing Polish equivalents in brackets. No disrespect is meant to the proud and historic Polish naming system but it was found that changes made after the war to both the road layout and the administrative districts means that modern locales would have detracted from the overall narrative. The intention is that we give the reader the best possible understanding of events in Poland in early 1945.

Daniel Taylor, Editor

THE SOVIET DASH TO THE ODER

ON 12TH JANUARY 1945 the Soviet Red Army unleashed its winter offensive. The attack was on a broad front, either side of Warsaw with five army groups – from north to south the Third, Second and First Byelorussian Fronts and the First and Fourth Ukrainian Fronts. Within a few days they had overwhelmed Heeresgruppe A defending the line of the Vistula river and began streaming westwards.

In the sector commanded by Marshal of the Soviet Union Georgy Zhukov, the First Byelorussian Front, the 1st and 2nd Guards Tank Armies made good progress, almost unopposed as they began their dash across Poland. Following in their wake were several other armies, among them the 5th Shock and the 8th Guards. The speed of the advance was so great that in the last days of January the Soviet forces reached the Oder on a broad front and, in the following few days, established small bridgeheads on its western bank at Göritz and Kienitz near Küstrin and south of Frankfurt-an-der-Oder. Berlin, now lay just 60 kilometres away and was in immediate danger. However, that was the limit of the Soviet offensive. Their lines of supply were overstretched, the men were exhausted and their vehicles were in need of urgent maintenance and repair.

The lightning drive across Poland had brought panic on the German side. On 21st January, hoping to stem the tide, the Oberkommando des Heeres[1] created a new army group, Heeresgruppe Weichsel, Hitler appointing Reichsführer-SS Heinrich Himmler as its commander on the 26th. Its task was to defend Pomerania and the Oder line northwards from Küstrin. On 25th January, in response to the Russian threat, a number of cities along the Oder were declared as Festungen (fortresses): – Frankfurt-an-der-Oder, Glogau, Breslau, Ratibor and Küstrin, They were tasked with stopping the Soviet advance on the river, the last natural obstacle before Berlin.

On their way the Soviet forces had bypassed pockets of enemy resistance. Many were to be mopped up by the following units but one was too big to be dealt with so easily. The fortress city of Posen. Soon the fortifications which had been erected many decades before were to be tested.

---

1. German Army High Command, usually abbreviated as OKH

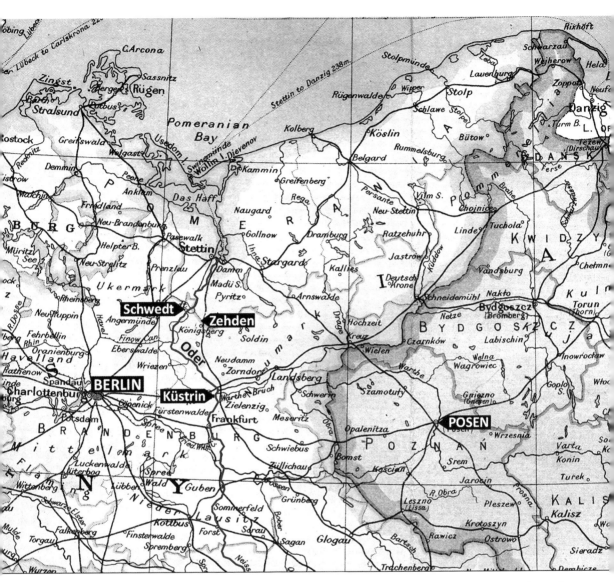

Europe as it appeared in 1939, before western Poland was absorbed by Germany. In late January 1945 the Soviet Red Army first encircled and then laid siege to the Polish city of Poznan in western Poland. The Germans, who judged Poznan, or Posen as they called it, very much a German city (it had formed part of Prussia for over a century), decided to defend it as a Festung (fortress), the aim of their stand being to hamper the advance of the Soviet armies streaming past on either side. It took a full month of heavy and costly fighting before the Russians finally managed to reduce Festung Posen. With the Wehrmacht retreating back into Germany before the Soviet onslaught, the German high command also ordered that bridgeheads be maintained on the eastern bank of the Oder river. One of the main bridgeheads was at Schwedt, with a smaller one some 25 kilometres to the south at Zehden. The Oder bridgeheads lay just 60 kilometres from Berlin. From late January to the end of March 1945, the German city of Küstrin, located at the confluence of the Oder and Warthe rivers, held out against the Red Army onslaught, forming a major obstacle for the planned Soviet advance to Berlin. Küstrin is located 65 kilometres due east of Berlin. Reichsstrasse 1 and a main railway line connected the two cities. After the war, with Poland being shifted westwards as a result of the 1945 Potsdam Conference and the Oder becoming the new German-Polish border, Schwedt (on the river's west bank) became a frontier town and Zehden (on the east side of the river) ended up in Poland, being renamed Cedynia.

The Soviet Dash to the Oder • 9

PART I.
FESTUNG POSEN

GERMAN SIEGE PREPARATIONS

The Germans had already started preparing to defend the city in the autumn of 1944. The first line of defence was planned to run around the city at a radius of 25 kilometres from its centre. Some 160 kilometres long, it never got beyond the planning stage as the Germans had neither the manpower to build it nor the troops to man it. The second line, drawn at a distance of 12 to 15 kilometres from the city, had a length of 100 kilometres and was to consist not only of field fortifications but also of Ringstand 58c bunkers[2]. It never fully materialised but of the works that were completed, most were located east of the city.

The third and final line was based on the perimeter of the eighteen forts and several dozen small bunkers. It consisted of foxholes, machine-gun posts and trenches connecting the forts and other fortified structures. An

2. The classic 'Tobruk' style machine-gun emplacement.

The city of Poznan (Posen in German) lies in the region known as Wielkopolska (Greater Poland) in western Poland, which is regarded by Poles as the heartland of the Polish nation, situated on the banks of the Warta (Warthe) river. From the early beginnings of the Polish state Poznan was one of the most important of its strongholds and the seat of its kings and princes. Its location on the Central European east-west axis and at the junction of major trade routes was a source of its wealth and growing importance through the centuries. On the other hand, this key position also made it liable to invasion from both east and west. In due course the city lost its political importance but it always remained a major economic centre.

In the wake of the partitions of Poland at the end of the 18th century, Wielkopolska became one of the provinces of Prussia, with Poznan as its capital. The new rulers soon decided that the city should be fortified, both to block the shortest route of advance by Russian forces towards Berlin as well as to suppress Polish efforts to gain independence. Work began in 1828 and by the end of the 19th century the city was ringed by a set of 18 forts and with a large Citadel (Fort Winiary) just north of the Old Town. It represented the third-largest fortress system of its kind in Europe.

The Prussian rulers also made efforts to Germanise the region, particularly after the founding of the German Reich in 1871, and from 1886 onwards the Prussian Settlement Commission was active in increasing German land ownership in formerly Polish areas.

Following the end of the First World War, after more than a century of foreign rule, the Poles gained their independence as a result of the ▼

Having invaded Poland in September 1939, the Germans soon made Poznan the capital of their Reichsgau Wartheland, a new province created after the annexation of western Poland to the Reich. The city's name reverted to Posen and Arthur Greiser was appointed Gauleiter of the new region. For the next five years he ruled with an iron fist, exploiting the economy, terrorising the Poles, persecuting the Jews, and introducing German colonists to germanise the region. Greiser set up his residence in the Imperial Castle (Kaiser-Schloss). Hitler ordered that the castle was to be his official residence which led to much of its interior being remodelled along Nazi lines. Here Greiser (right) is reviewing troops outside the castle in November 1939. With him are Reich Minister Wilhelm Frick, and General Walter Petzel, the commander of Wehrkreis XXI (Posen), the newly-created army district in the new Gau.
(BA Bild 183-E12078)

The later alteration of the castle along Nazi architectural lines also affected the exterior as can be clearly seen from the re-styled entrance.
(Tomasz Zgoda)

The Soviet Dash to the Oder • 11

Treaty of Versailles in 1919. The success of the Wielkopolskie Uprising of 1918-19 ensured that most of that region and Poznan became part of the new state.

On 1st September, 1939, after just 20 years of independence, Poland was attacked by Nazi Germany and the Soviet Union, and was partitioned once again. Poznan was occupied without a fight by Wehrmacht troops on 10th September after the Polish Poznan Army had abandoned it and moved eastwards to avoid encirclement.

Following the German-Russian occupation, Poland was carved up into three parts: the eastern half was annexed by the Soviet Union; the middle part became the so-called Generalgouvernement under German rule, and the western provinces were annexed by Germany and became part of the German Reich. The annexed districts formed three new Reichsgaue (administrative and party districts): Danzig-Westpreussen, Wartheland (with Posen as its capital) and Oberschlesien, each governed by a Reichsstatthalter/Gauleiter. The new head of the Wartheland district was SS-Obergruppenführer Arthur Greiser, who quickly established himself in Poznan, setting up his residence in the Kaiser-Schloss (Zamek Cesarski), the imperial castle built by Kaiser Wilhelm II in 1905-10.

In the following years the city played a crucial role in the German war effort, both as a road and rail junction and as a supply centre for the Eastern Front. Like other cities in Poland, the city suffered cruelly under German occupation. Around 100,000 of its Polish inhabitants – one-third of its population – were expelled to the Generalgouvernement and an estimated 10,000 perished in German concentration camps. Thousands of others (mostly intelligentsia, scientists, participants of the 1918-19 insurgency, etc.) were killed in the notorious Fort VII on the western outskirts and at other places in the city. Many more were condemned to forced labour.

At the same time, Greiser's administration set about imposing German hegemony on the region and the city. Poznan was renamed Posen and all city districts, all streets and all landmark buildings received German names. All signs of Polish presence and culture in town and region were to be erased. In the place of the Poles that had been expelled came tens of thousands of ethnic Germans from the Baltic States, Volhylnia, Eastern Galicia, the Ukraine and elsewhere. This Germanisation campaign was systematically pursued throughout the occupation but had to be abandoned as the Eastern Front approached the borders of the Third Reich.

anti-tank ditch barred the entrance to the city though it was not finished everywhere. The last point of resistance was the Citadel, or Kernwerk as the Germans called it, which was situated on the hill immediately north of the Old Town. Though built in the 19th century and by now outdated, the forts offered some form of protection against most of the Soviet artillery as well as from the cold. Each of the city's forts also served as warehouses for uniforms, equipment, arms and ammunition.

The city itself could be used for defence to a varying degree. The districts of Oststadt and Heinrichstadt, located north-east and east of the Warthe river, were densely built up, thus offering the Germans good conditions for defence, while the Bamberg and Louisenhain districts, located in the south-eastern part of the city, consisted of small farms and isolated houses scattered in open fields, which potentially gave an attacker easy access to the city from this direction.

On 16th October 1944, Adolf Hitler decreed the creation of the Volkssturm, conscripting all males between the ages of 16 and 60 years who were not already serving in some military unit. Volkssturm militias, consisting mainly of old men and Hitlerjugend teenagers, were raised in all towns and cities within the Reich. Here members of the Posen Volkssturm parade past Reichsführer-SS Heinrich Himmler on Schlossfreiheit, the street passing in front of Poznan's Imperial Palace, in October 1944. Taking the salute with Himmler from the SdKfz 7 heavy half-track are Gauleiter Greiser (left) and Generaloberst Heinz Guderian, the Chief of the OKH General Staff (right). (NAC/ADM)

Schlossfreiheit is today named Adam Mickiewicz Square, and where the half-track was set up now stands the monument commemorating the anti-Soviet demonstrations that occurred in Poznan in June 1956. Begun as a general strike for better work conditions in the Joseph Stalin Metal Works on 28th June, the protest quickly developed into a mass demonstration against the dictatorial regime of the Communist rulers. A crowd of 100,000 assembled in front of the Imperial Palace and protesters attacked and occupied party, government and secret police buildings. That same afternoon a force of 400 tanks and 10,000 troops of the Polish People's Army and the Interior Security Corps entered the city and violently suppressed the uprising. At least 57 people were killed, with some 600 others wounded and over 700 detained. 'Poznan June' was the first of a series of anti-Soviet mass protests that rocked the Polish People's Republic in the summer and autumn of 1956, leading to the installation of a less hard-line Stalinist government under Wladyslaw Gomulka in October of that year. The monument, designed by sculptor Adam Graczyk and architect Wlodzimierz Wojciechowski, was unveiled in June 1981, the 25th anniversary of the uprising. (Tomasz Zgoda)

The city of Posen as it was under German control. In order to orientate the visitor to modern metropolis that is Poznan, here are the comparative locations shown in the text. The destruction of the city and a different method of administration mean that there is not always a perfect comparison.

Districts

German	Polish
Altstadt	Stare Miasto
Bahn-in-Pommern	Banie
Bamberg	Zegrze & Rataje
Benschen	Zbaszyn
Bolchau	Bolechów
Breslau	Wroclaw
Kernwerk	Fort Winiary (Citadel)
Dembsen	Debiec
Golnau	Golecin
Gunterhausen	Naramowice
Heinrichstadt	Osiedle & Sródka
Hermannstadt	Lazarze
Jerzitz	Jezyce
Johannistal	Berdychowo
Kreising	Krzesiny
Lenzingen	Gorczyn
Louisenhain	Staroleka
Lobau	Lubon
Obernick	Oborniki
Oststadt	Glówna & Zawady
Pyritz	Pyrzyce
Seehof	Antoninek
Städtchen	Miasteczko
Staffelbach	Czapury
Steineck	Lawica
Treskau	Owinska
Weinern	Winiary, Winogrady & Szelag
Wilde	Wilda

Street Names

Adalbertstrasse	Świętego Wojciecha
Bambergerstrasse	Dolna Wilda
Bayernstrasse	Niestachowska
Berlinerstrasse	Grudnia
Bismarckstrasse	Kantaka
Breitestrasse	Wielka
Burggrafenring	Wały Królowej Jadwigi
Dietrich-Eckartstrasse	Libelta
Kaiser-Ring	Waly Leszczynskiego
Leo-Schlageterstrasse	Mielzynskiego
Magazinstrasse	Solna Street
Martinstrasse	Swietego Marcin
Nieder-Wall	Waly Zygmunta Augusta
Pirscherstrasse	Przecznica
Saarlandstrasse	Dabrowskiego
Tiergartenstrasse	Zwierzyniecka
Wallischei	Chwaliszewo
Warschauerstrasse	Warszawska

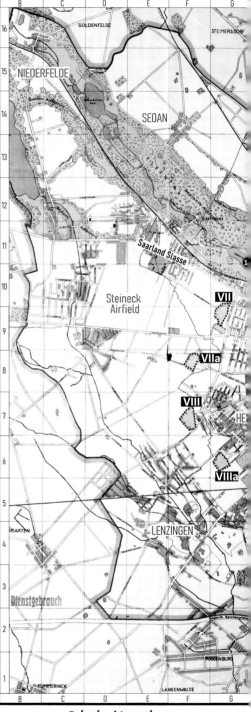

Principal Locations

❶ Horst-Wessel-Platz   Rynek Wildecki
❷ Kaiser-Schloss   Zamek Cesarski
   Imperial Palace
❸ Wallischei-Brücke   Chwaliszewski Bridge
❹ Kernwerk   Citadel
❺ Fort Prittwitz.
❻ Fort Radziwill
❼ Fort Rauch
❽ Fort Grolman

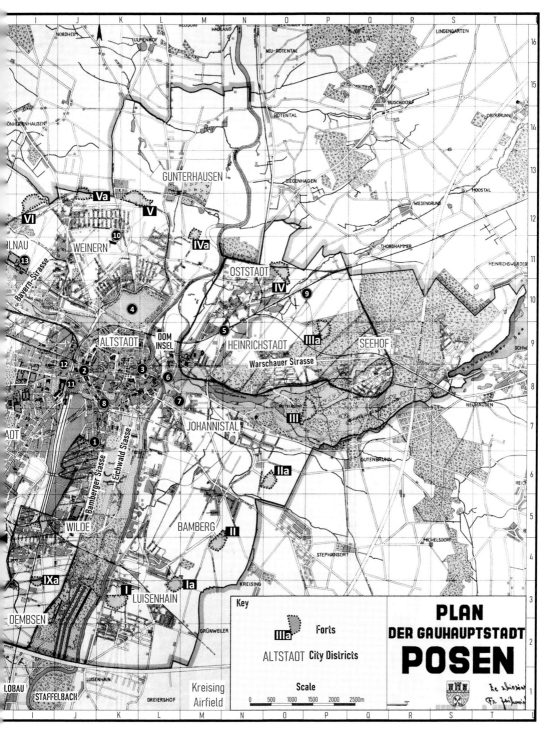

- ⑨ 'Flak-Höhe'
  Flak Heights
- ⑩ Zeppelinwiese
- ⑪ Hauptbahnhof
  Main Railway Station
- ⑫ Reichs-Universität Posen
  Poznan University
- ⑬ Kuhndorf barracks
- ⑭ Elsen-See *Rusalka Lake*

A rare wartime German map of Posen. During their five-year reign, the Nazi authorities introduced German names for all streets in the city and for all of the administrative districts. As these were the names in use at the time, they have been used in the narrative of this book – the captions then show German names for wartime locations and Polish names to accompany their modern comparisons. The eighteen forts that ringed the city have been marked with Roman numerals. The various districts and some roads have also been labelled for clarity.

These Volkssturm troopers on Martin-Strasse (the continuation of Schlossfreiheit) are pulling MG 151/20 machine guns, a type produced in the local arms factories of the Deutsche Waffen und Munitionsfabrik. The building in the background is the University Hall of the Poznan University, known under German rule as the Reichsuniversität Posen. This building would become a heavily-contested bastion during the battle for the city three months later. (NAC/ADM)

Since 1955 the university has been known as the Adam Mickiewicz University after Poland's greatest poet (1798-1855). As for the machine guns, it is a peculiarity of history that the Deutsche Waffen und Munitionsfabrik, from which they came, later became the Joseph Stalin Metal Works from which the anti-Soviet uprising of 1956 emanated. (Tomasz Zgoda)

16 • RED ARMY TOWARDS THE ODER – THEN AND NOW

The districts west of the Warthe were more-densely built up. However, the two southern districts Wilde and Dembsen, where the buildings were more widely dispersed, offered the easiest access to the city centre. A line of monumental public buildings located on the site of the former Prussian ramparts favoured the defenders if the attacker was able to penetrate up to this point. The Altstadt, or Old Town, offered good opportunities to set up a defence within the walls of its stoutly built, though elderly buildings.

The Warthe river remained frozen for most of the month-long battle, providing both sides with the opportunity to cross it on foot.

The German strategy was to hold the city as a Festung (fortress) and have it serve the role of a 'Wellenbrecher' (breakwater). The aim was to let the enemy encircle the city and engage him in a protracted siege that would prevent him from concentrating his additional forces further west along the Oder in the area of Küstrin and for a later offensive towards Berlin. The other objective was to hold the city's important road and railway junctions for as long as possible in order to deny the enemy the best methods to supply his advancing armies.

ALARM!

Sirens wailed throughout Festung Posen at 0525-hrs on 20th January 1945. Generalmajor Ernst Mattern, the commander of the Warthelager, the large Wehrmacht training ground to the north of the city, had been appointed Festungskommandant (Fortress Commander). He quickly ordered the evacuation of all civilians from the city. However, despite the approaching battle, many of the inhabitants decided to stay, and an estimated 100,000 Poles plus an unknown number of the German population remained in the city. In addition to the civilian evacuation, Gauleiter Greiser and all Nazi Party and German administrative authorities abandoned the city.

The force that defended Posen included many second-line and training units that had been part of the city's regular garrison before the battle. They were composed of the instructors and infantry officer cadets of the Schule V für Fahnenjunker der Infanterie – some 1,300 men in all. The cadets were all given the rank of Leutnant and would form the core of the lower cadre in the defence units. Of the more regular army units, the defence included an assault gun training unit, Sturmgeschütz-Ersatz und Ausbildungs-Abteilung 500, and several fortress units: Festungs-Pak-Abteilung 102 (anti-tank), Festungs-MG-Bataillone 82 and 83 (machine gun), Festung-Pionier-Kompanie 66 (engineers) and Festungs-Bataillon 1446. In addition, there were four Landesschützen-Bataillone 21, 312, 475 and 647 – the town's home guard, two garrison units (Standort-Bataillon z.b.V.[3] and Dolmetscher-Abteilung XXI) and one militia unit, Volkssturm-Bataillon 15, one of four such battalions originally raised by the city.

Three battalions were made up of Luftwaffe personnel. Formed out of Flieger-Ersatz-und-Ausbildungs-Abteilung 1 and many smaller air force units,

---

3. The abbreviation z.b.V. stands for zur besonderen Verwendung, - a 'unit for special use'.

which were formed into Bataillon Rogalsky (named after its commander, Oberstleutnant Fritz Rogalsky), Bataillon Degive (Major Carl Degive) and one battalion whose commander's name is not known.

Finally, there were SS-Kampfgruppe Lenzer, made up of all the SS personnel found in the city, and Polizei-Regiment Schallert, comprising three company-size units formed from the city's police. In addition, there were various smaller units consisting of members of the Reichsarbeitsdienst[4], Organisation Todt, fire service, air raid service and other rear-echelon troops.

The garrison's artillery included eight field artillery batteries with a combined strength of thirty-eight guns, and Flak-Untergruppe Posen armed with thirty-two 8.8cm heavy anti-aircraft and eighty-eight light (3.7mm and 2cm) anti-aircraft guns.

A powerful element of the garrison was the so-called Panzer-Stoss-Reserve (Armoured Assault Reserve), commanded by Hauptmann Wolf von Malotki and consisting of one Tiger I, two Panthers, one PzKpfw IV, one Hetzer tank destroyer, a self-propelled gun of an unknown type and around eighteen StuGs and StuH 42s, the latter provided by Sturmgeschütz-Ersatz und Ausbildungs-Abteilung 500.

It was these forces – some 8,000 to 10,000 men in all – that formed the core of the city garrison. According to the German plans, they were to be reinforced by Wehrmacht forces retreating from the east. From 20th February special collecting units started gathering every man that came in from the east. However, many of the latter, knowing what fate would await them if they got holed up in the city, avoided getting ensnared. As it was, the only sizable forces that reinforced the garrison were Kampfgruppe Uhlig, comprising the remnants of the 251. Infanterie-Division; an infantry training battalion, Infanterie-Ersatz- und Ausbildungs-Abteilung 67; an anti-aircraft battery, RAD-Doppel-Batterie, armed with six 8.8cm and two 2cm FlaK guns; plus a battalion of Hungarian officer cadets. These newly arrived troops added a further 3,000 to 4,000 soldiers.

In total, this meant that the city had managed to amass an estimated 15,000 to 20,000 men for its defence. They were organised into new units and divided over the various defence sectors as follows:

Sector East (Abschnitt Ost) commanded by Oberst Ernst Gonell:
- subsector I: Bataillon Werner and Bataillon Schomaker (later Pfeiffer),
- subsector II: Bataillon von den Driesch and Bataillon Koch,
- subsector III: Bataillon Styx and Bataillon Hamel,
- Reserve-Bataillon Ost/Kampfgruppe Schulte (later Säger)
- six artillery batteries and part of Festungs-Pak-Abteilung 102.

Sector West (Abschnitt West) under Major Heinz Martin Ewert
- subsector IV North (Unterabschnitt Nord): Bataillon Prasser and Bataillon Zaag (later Fütterer)
- subsector V West and South (Unterabschnitt West und Süd): Volkssturm-Bataillon 15, Luftwaffe-Bataillon Degive, Luftwaffe-

---

4. RAD – the Reich labour service

Bataillon Rogalsky, Kampfgruppe Uhlig, SS-Kampfgruppe Lenzer, seven artillery batteries and many smaller infantry units.

Sector Warthe (Abschnitt Warthe) led by Major Eberhard Hahn:
 • Landesschützen-Bataillone 475 and 647, two reserve infantry companies and part of Festungs-Pak-Abteilung 102, divided between subsectors North and South (Unterabschnitt Nord and Unterabschnitt Süd).

Reserve of the Festungskommandant:
 • the armour of the Panzer-Stoss-Reserve and many smaller infantry units.

RED ARMY AT THE GATES

22nd to 25th January
On 22nd January spearheads of Major-General Ivan Dremov's 8th Guards Mechanised Corps – the vanguard of Colonel-General Mikhail Katukov's 1st Guards Tank Army – appeared in the suburbs of Posen. Three of its formations attacked towards the city. Tanks from the 21st Guards Mechanised Brigade were assigned to take the south-eastern districts of Städtchen, Bamberg and Louisenhain, whilst the 1st Guards Armoured Brigade was to attack towards the eastern district of Heinrichstadt, and the 19th Guards Mechanised Brigade had orders to take the north-eastern district of Oststadt. The corps' fourth formation, the 20th Guards Mechanised Brigade, was ordered to outflank the city to the south and cross the river Warthe.

Meanwhile, north of the city, units of Colonel Hamazasp Babadzhanian's 11th Guards Armoured Corps – also from Katukov's 1st Guards Tank Army – attempted to capture bridges over the Warthe but stubborn German defence prevented this. Resistance was met near the village of Bolchau, 16 kilometres north of the city, and then at the town of Obernick, another 15 kilometres further north. Finally, on 24th January, infantry of the 40th and 45th Guards Armoured Brigades were able to cross the river near the village of Treskau, 12 kilometres north of the city, and they rapidly created a bridgehead on the west bank.

Efforts south of Posen proved more successful where the 20th Guards Mechanised Brigade was able to capture the Focke-Wulf aircraft factory and the nearby airfield at Kreising. With the help of Polish civilian guides, they then managed to reach the Warthe near the village of Staffelbach, four kilometres south of the city. Reconnaissance units quickly crossed the frozen river with light vehicles and guns and established a small bridgehead on the west bank. The German unit guarding that sector, Luftwaffe-Bataillon Rogalsky, abandoned its positions and retreated towards the city, enabling the Soviets an undisturbed reinforcement of their bridgehead. The Luftwaffe unit also failed to inform the Festung command about the crossing, delaying any German counter-moves.

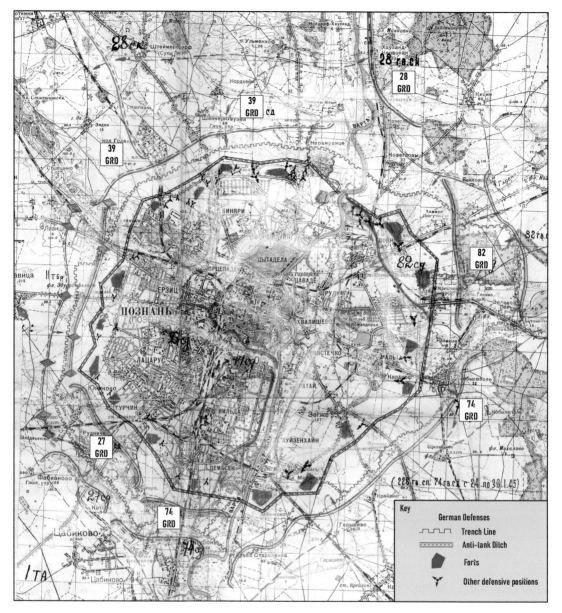

Original Russian map from the records of the First Byelorussian Front showing the ring formed around the city by the five infantry divisions of the 8th Guards Army: clockwise, from the top, the 39th, 28th, 82nd, 74th and 27th Guards Rifle Divisions. Fighting a concentric battle is complicated - as your forces squeeze in on an enemy location, room for manoeuvre diminishes and there is the heightened chance of your own forces shooting on one another. The phase lines just visible on this map demonstrate how areas were designated to each division.

When Generalmajor Mattern finally learned of the crossing, he immediately despatched Luftwaffe aircraft from the Steineck aerodrome, west of the city, with orders to destroy the enemy's bridges. However, these did not stop the Soviet crossings. To prevent further air attacks, a small detachment from the 21st Guards Mechanised Brigade – three tanks and four armoured personnel carriers – was sent to capture Steineck. Their sudden appearance completely surprised the Germans who panicked and blew up aircraft and airfield installations.

During the first days of the encirclement of Posen, the way to the west was deliberately left open by the 88th Guards Rifle Division (Major-General Boris Pankov) supported by the 11th Guards Heavy Tank Brigade. Their goal was to lure the Germans into open terrain in order to ambush them there and avoid costly street-fighting. This proved to be futile, the Germans having clearly seen through the Russian ploy, and the 88th Guards Rifle Division left this area on 31st January.

On 24th January, the 1st Guards Armoured Brigade and 19th Guards Mechanised Brigade crossed the Warthe near Staffelbach, joining the 20th and 21st Guards Mechanised Brigades in the bridgehead. The following day, the whole 8th Guards Mechanised Corps started leaving the southern outskirts of Posen in the direction of the Oder river.

SOVIET SUBSTITUTION

The task of capturing the city was now handed over to two corps of Colonel-General Vasily Chuikov's 8th Guards Army and one corps of Colonel-General Vladimir Kolpakchy's 69th Army. The 29th Guards Rifle Corps of Major-General Afanasi Shemenkov comprised the 27th, 74th and 82nd Guards Rifle Divisions; the 28th Guards Rifle Corps, commanded by Lieutenant-General Alexander Ryzhov, provided the 39th Guards Rifle Division, and the 91st Rifle Corps (69th Army), led by Lieutenant-General Fedor Volkov, fielded the 117th and 312th Rifle Divisions. These six infantry divisions were supported by one armoured brigade and eight armoured regiments as well as by eleven artillery brigades and four artillery regiments. The Soviets had a small advantage over the Germans in infantry but their superiority in artillery, tanks and ground-support aircraft was overwhelming.

The 27th Guards Rifle Division (Major-General Viktor Glebov) and 74th Guards Rifle Division (Major-General Dmitri Bakanov) moved across the Warthe into the Staffelbach bridgehead with orders to attack towards the city centre from the south and south-west; the 312th Rifle Division (Major-General Aleksandr Moiseyevski) would fight on both banks of the river south of the city; the 82nd Guards Rifle Division (Major-General Georgi Khetagurov) and 117th Rifle Division (Major-General Ermolai Koberidze) surrounded the city from the east and the 39th Guards Rifle Division (Colonel Efim Marchenko) was deployed north of the city with the objective of attacking south towards the two divisions of the 28th Corps.

THE SOUTHERN AND WESTERN DISTRICTS

26th January to 3rd February

Realising that the southern part of the fortress perimeter was held by Luftwaffe units, who were poorly trained for ground combat, the Soviet command decided to take advantage of this and strike at this sector first. On 26th January, the 74th and 27th Guards Rifle Divisions attacked, the

The attack into the city began on 26th January and came in from the south, the 74th and 27th Guards Rifle Divisions attacking side by side. Supporting the two divisions was the 34th Independent Guards Heavy Tank Regiment, commanded by Lieutenant-Colonel Michail Oglobin. Here a column of their IS-2 tanks has halted on Schwaben-Strasse (Górna Wilda Street), just south of Rynek Wildecki, the market square in the district of Wilda, known during the German occupation as Horst-Wessel-Platz. This was in the operational zone of the 74th Guards Rifle Division. (Soviet Newsreel)

Schwaben-Strasse is today known as Ulica 28 Czerwca 1956 Roku (Street of 28 June 1956), another reminder of the uprising of 1956. The view is north, towards Wildecki Market, with Kilinskiego Street on the left. (Tomasz Zgoda)

22 • RED ARMY TOWARDS THE ODER – THEN AND NOW

former with its right flank on the Warthe river and aiming for the Dembsen and Wilde districts, and the latter from south of the Posen–Berlin railway line and striking northwards towards the Dembsen and Hermannstadt districts. Soon the suburb of Lobau was taken from the hands of Luftwaffe-Bataillon Rogalsky, which was pushed back towards Fort IXa. The latter was soon surrounded by the 74th Guards Rifle Division and forced to surrender encouraged by the use of flame-throwers and explosives. Capture of the fort was made easier due to the fact that part of its moat had been filled in when the railway from Posen to Breslau, which ran immediately to the west of it, was built.

Heavy fighting also raged west of this railway line. Members of Battalions Degive and Rogalsky were pushed back towards Dembsen, Hermanstadt and Fort IX. Troops of Glebov's 27th Guards Rifle Division tried to take the fort with the help of tanks but this assault was repulsed.

Making use of the collapse of the German defensive line south of the city, Glebov's troops, advanced past Fort IX on 27th January, as far as the Humbold-Platz. The fort itself also fell that day. The southern part of the Hermanstadt district fell into Russian hands the following day. Fierce fighting raged throughout the western districts of the city.

Bakanov's 74th Guards Rifle Division, on the right, renewed its attack towards the forest that lies between Fort IXa and the Warthe, which was defended by the RAD-Flak-Batterie and Landesschützen-Bataillon 475. The German 88mm guns soon fell silent due to lack of ammunition and were destroyed. Pushing the German forces back towards the city, Bakanov's troops advanced through the Wilde district and neared the Horst-Wessel-Platz (Rynek Wildecki). Here the leading IS-2 tanks from the 34th Guards Heavy Tank Regiment were confronted by a Panther tank but it proved to have been abandoned by its crew. The loss of two forts and the wholesale defeat of the defenders in this sector proved crippling for the Festung.

The Germans launched two counter-attacks in order to stop the Soviet advance towards the city centre and restore the previous front line. The first attempt was made with infantry alone in the area from the Warthe to Bamberger Strasse. Lacking support, it failed. The second attempt was more concerted. It was carried out by the Panzer-Stoss-Reserve with around eleven Sturmgeschütze towing 2cm cannons on sledges accompanied by a single Panther tank. Infantry support was provided by cadets of the Fahnenjunker-Schule advancing southwards from Eichwald-Strasse to its junction with Bamberger Strasse. Unfortunately for the Germans they failed to notice that the buildings further north along Bamberger Strasse were occupied by Soviet infantry supported by anti-tank guns. To make matters worse, the route of attack was poorly chosen as the ground around Eichwald-Strasse was at that time exceedingly soft and offered little opportunity to deploy the armoured vehicles off the road. The Germans also did not know that Red Army troops had blocked the tunnel below the railway embankment.

As they approached Horst-Wessel-Platz on 27th January, the tanks of the 34th Tank Regiment were confronted by a German Panther that appeared to be guarding the square. It belonged to the so-called Panzer-Stoss-Reserve (Armoured Assault Reserve), the force of tanks and assault guns that served as the Festung's 'fire brigade' during the defence of the city. There are conflicting accounts of how it came to its end here. One version says a Polish civilian guided the IS-2 tanks through the maze of streets, enabling one to approach the Panther from the rear and knock it out with two rounds through the front armour. Another indicates that the Panther had taken part in the German counter-attack in southern Posen earlier that day during which it had received two hits on the frontal armour, which did not penetrate but wounded the tank commander, Hauptmann Wolf von Malotki (who also commanded the Panzer-Stoss-Reserve). The Panther had then moved (or been towed back) to this spot on Horst-Wessel-Platz where it had then been abandoned by the crew, possibly because they knew the Russian armour was close behind. The latter version seems the more probable, especially since Polish witnesses who entered the interior afterwards say it was not damaged.

Wildecki Market has seen little change since the war. The church in the background is the Kosciól Maryi Królowej (Church of Queen Mary). The view is looking north, towards the city centre.
(Tomasz Zgoda)

24 • RED ARMY TOWARDS THE ODER – THEN AND NOW

Soon the first Sturmgeschütze and the Panther were hit, the other armoured vehicles then turned towards the Soviet positions along Bamberger Strasse. The supporting German infantry was targeted by Soviet machine guns and artillery. Nonetheless, in spite of all this, by the end of the day the Germans had pushed the 74th Guards Rifle Division back as far as the railway embankment. However, the Festung command soon decided to withdraw part of the Sturmgeschütz unit, leaving only three for the defence. At the end of the day the remaining assault guns were ordered back to the Citadel as they were short of ammunition and had no cover from the right flank due to the shortage of men. The day's effort had proved to be a costly, though ultimately fruitless, victory for the Germans. They managed to postpone the Russian offensive for just one day at the cost of three assault guns destroyed.

On 28th January the two divisions of the 29th Guards Rifle Corps advanced even further towards the city centre. Glebov's 27th Guards Rifle Division waged street battles in the north of the Hermanstadt district and Bakanov's 74th Guards Rifle Division fought for Fort Grolman, one of the four older forts protecting the inner city, and the area to the east of there. Meanwhile, Marchenko's 39th Guards Rifle Division of the 28th Guards Rifle Corps, which was coming towards them from the north side of the city, was penetrating into the northern part of the Jersitz district and reached the Botanic Gardens.

The following day, January 29, the 27th Guards Rifle Division reached the southern part of Jersitz. Street-fighting raged there and in the woodland to the north. There was no fixed front line and both sides fought for every house in desperate hand-to-hand combat. Fort VIIIa, located to the south-west of Hermanstadt was now cut off from the city. By evening the troops in the fort had surrendered. From 30th January to 2nd February, the 39th Guards Rifle Division, arriving from the north and turning its advance from south to east, gradually pushed the Germans eastwards along Saarland-Strasse. To slow the Russian onslaught, the Germans blew up the Theater-Brücke, one of the viaducts over the railway line giving access to the Old Town from the west.

By 31st January, the situation for the German troops bottled up in Forts VII, VIIa and VIII, had become acute. Located on the western and south-western edge of the city, the Soviet troops surrounded them. At last, the defenders received orders to break out and head towards the Citadel. Apparently, the commanders of these forts were no longer willing to remain in the encircled city. Instead they ordered their troops to head westward in the hope of reaching the German positions along the Oder and Neisse rivers in Pomerania. Few managed to reach safety.

On 1st February, the International Fair complex, part of the Hauptbahnhof (main railway station) and the area of Pirscher-Strasse and Tiergarten-Strasse were lost to the 27th Guards Rifle Division. The area was important because just east of it lay another viaduct across the railway giving access to the Old Town. By 3rd February, the 39th Guards Rifle Division had captured all of the Jersitz district and most of the Main Railway Station. Organised German resistance west and south of the Old Town effectively ceased.

The tank crews of the 34th Guards Heavy Tank Regiment were warmly welcomed by the Polish citizens on Schwaben-Strasse – in stark contrast to what would happen eleven years later.

Looking north on Ulica 28 Czerwca 1956 Roku today. This part of Posen has seen very little change since the war. The damage to the house on the left has been repaired.

More scenes of rejoicing. The spot where the Panther stood is just a few hundred metres further up the street.
(RGAKFiD)

The same view in 2019, with Krzyzowa Street on the right and Wildecki Market just around the corner on the left.
(Tomasz Zgoda)

Part I. Festung Posen • 27

The crew of a 76.2mm ZIS-3 anti-tank gun in action, its barrel is pointing north into Schwaben-Strasse (Górna Wilda Street). Note the white sheet hung over the gun shield as winter camouflage. The crew member on the left has German Mauser ammo pouches on his belt – by this time of the war it was common to see Russian soldiers utilising items from German uniforms and equipment.

Looking into Wierzbiecice Street (Langemarck-Strasse) from the northern end of Wildecki Market. (Tomasz Zgoda)

THE NORTHERN DISTRICTS

26th January to 16th February

The first troops of the 39th Guards Rifle Division had appeared in villages north of Posen on 26th January. Their sector of the front line stretched from Saarland-Strasse in the west to the suburb village of Guntershausen in the north. The following day, 27th January, the division attacked along its entire line. German resistance was stiff and the assault was stopped in front of the anti-tank ditch. Next day brought only a minor Soviet incursion in the area south of the Kuhndorf military barracks, which was soon repelled thanks to a counter-attack by Kampfgruppe Lohse. However, a Soviet attack launched towards the area of the Elsen-See and the Dom Dobrego Pasterza Convent completely decimated the Hungarian battalion defending there. The line had to be restored with the help of the Tiger I and a Panzer IV from the Panzer-Stoss-Reserve with assistance from various other infantry units.

Another assault by the 39th Division north of Elsen-See launched on 29th January was more successful and penetrated the German lines as far as Bayern-Strasse. Neither side occupied the Kuhndorf barracks, which consisted of several stoutly-built brick barrack blocks and was seemingly well suited for defence. They lay in relatively open ground and so perhaps reaching them – and more particularly the difficulty of withdrawing from them – made them unattractive?

During the night of 30th/31st January Khetagurov's 82nd Guards Rifle Division (29th Guards Rifle Corps) was withdrawn from its previous

The Russian advance into the city was particularly well supported by artillery. Here a 122mm M1938 (M-30) howitzer supports the advance of the 27th Guards Rifle Division from Richthofen-Allee (Hetmanska Street), the east-west road separating the Górczyn and Lazarz districts. (Soviet Newsreel)

This area was completely transformed after the war. Only the steeple of the Church of Our Lady of Sorrows on Glogovska Street (Glogauer Strasse during the war) – albeit rebuilt – makes it possible to pinpoint the spot. (Tomasz Zgoda)

Part I. Festung Posen • **29**

By the end of the fourth day, the 74th Guards Rifle Division had reached the southern edge of the Old Town. Here men of the 1st Battalion of its 226th Regiment charge past buildings on Burggrafen-Ring (Waly Królowej Jadwigi Avenue). The sturdy buildings along this avenue formed the bulwark of the German defence in this sector. (RGAKFiD)

The right-hand building at No. 62 has been rebuilt but its neighbour, which stands on the corner of Królowej Jadwigi and Polwiejska Streets, has been replaced with a modern building housing a branch of the Polski Bank. (Tomasz Zgoda)

positions east of the city and sent north with orders to relieve Rakhimov's 39th Guards Rifle Division. Its new task was to launch an assault towards the Gunterhausen district, with the intention of capturing the forts located north of the city and the Weinern district as far as the northern slopes of

Another Russian soldier wearing German Mauser ammo pouches, pictured at the same corner. His relaxed attitude makes one wonder if the previous photo was not a staged action shot.

Looking east down Królowej Jadwigi Avenue in 2019. (Tomasz Zgoda)

the Citadel. The 39th Division, having been temporarily withdrawn, departed towards the Oder early on 3rd February.

During the next few days, the Soviet offensive whittled away at the German defences north of the city. Pressing shortages of heavy weapons and ammunition made the task of holding the line impossible for the remaining German forces. By 2nd February, Forts Va, VI and VIa had become completely surrounded and cut off. The latter two were captured in the following few days but Fort Va held out until 16th February. Khetagurov's troops stormed this last bastion with support of heavy artillery almost as a rehearsal for the oncoming assault on the Citadel. The German defensive lines in Gunterhausen held but it was only a matter of time before this district was also lost to the attackers.

On 4th February Khetagurov's division broke through towards the so-called Zeppelinwiese, a former airship landing ground with a large,

Part I. Festung Posen • 31

disused hanger. The Germans had turned the field into a makeshift airstrip. Although Festung Posen was clearly doomed, it was still being re-supplied by air.

From 28th January to 5th February, scores of Ju 52 transport aircraft landed on the Zeppelinwiese, bringing in supplies and evacuating wounded. When Soviet forces got close to the airstrip it became impossible to continue landing but the garrison was still supplied by parachute drop. These airlifts began on 8th February and were continued until the 23rd. However, after 16th February even that method had to be abandoned and the only dropping zone that remained was in the area around the Citadel. It is unknown how many of these air drops actually reached their mark.

Over the next few days, Weinern district and Forts Va and IVa were heavily contested. On 7th February, the Germans launched a successful counter-attack to recapture the area east of the Zeppelinwiese. During this assault, Lieutenant-Colonel Veniamin Klepikov, commander of 246th Rifle Regiment of the 82nd Guards Rifle Division, was killed, and several other senior officers of the division were wounded. Another German attempt to recapture the Zeppelinwiese was made on the 9th but this was repulsed. In response to these counter-attacks, the 82nd Guards Rifle Division battered its way towards the northern slopes of the Citadel. The following day, 11th February, brought another loss for the defenders when the ferry near the power station, which had maintained contact between Unterabschnitt Nord and Abschnitt Ost, was sunk by a bomb.

On 13th February Fort IVa was surrounded by the 82nd Guards Rifle Division and captured the following day after heavy fighting. On the 15th the last remaining defenders of Unterabschnitt Nord, including those in Fort V, were ordered to break through towards the Citadel. However, so strong was the Soviet resistance that they never made it there; instead, they broke out northwards the following day in the hope of reaching the German lines in Pomerania. Most of them were killed during the attempt or captured by Russian or Polish soldiers. An even crueller fate befell the German wounded left behind in Forts IVa and V: they were burned alive by the Russians using flame-throwers.

THE EASTERN DISTRICTS

21st January 15th February

Right at the beginning of the battle a Soviet reconnaissance unit of the 8th Guards Mechanised Corps managed to take the feature known as 'Flak-Höhe' (Flak Heights) without a fight. This was a crucial hill on the eastern outskirts of the city that got its name from the anti-aircraft guns that were stationed on the plateau on its top. Quick action by Hauptmann August Koch, commander of Bataillon Koch, enabled the Germans to re-take the hill in a swift counter-attack. This action proved invaluable for holding this sector over the succeeding three weeks.

A Soviet soldier talking into a field phone on the crossroads of Glogauer Strasse (Marszalka Focha Street) and Buker-Strasse (Bukowska Street), immediately west of the Old Town. This was in the sector of the 27th Guards Rifle Division.

The following day, 22nd January, the 1st Guards Armoured Brigade attacked from the east towards Seehof, an outlying housing estate along the main road from Warsaw. However, its commander was not aware that the Germans had placed two batteries of 8.8cm guns – schwere Flak-Batterieen 210 and 211 – on the hill and the Soviet assault, even with support of a number of T-34 tanks, was stopped in its tracks. Fighting also raged in the area of Fort IV, to the north of the Flak-Höhe, but the German line here held as well. Having had their nose bloodied, the units of the 8th Guards Mechanised Corps refrained from other attempts to pierce the German positions east of the Warthe until they were relieved by Khetagurov's 82nd Guards Rifle Division (of the 8th Guards Army's 29th Guards Rifle Corps) and the Koberidze's 117th and Moiseyevski's 312th Rifle Divisions (of the 69th Army's 91st Rifle Corps).

Marszalka Focha Street was re-named Roosevelta Street in honour of US President Franklin D. Roosevelt in November 1945. Bukowska Street was known as Karola Swierczewskiego Street until 1990 when it regained its old name Bukowska. The Baltyk Cinema that stood on the junction's northern corner since 1929 was pulled down in 2003 and a skyscraper, the Baltic Business Service Centre, today takes its place. (RGAKFiD)

Subsequently the eastern districts were relatively quiet compared to the

Part I. Festung Posen • 33

In the early morning of 31st January, assault groups of the 27th Guards Rifle Division, supported by two T-34/85 tanks from the 250th Independent Tank Regiment, broke into the Old Town from the west and ferocious fighting began on Schlossfreiheit and Martin-Strasse, the streets where the Volkssturm had paraded for Himmler three months before, both sides battling for possession of the University Hall, the Imperial Castle and the building of the Landgenossenschaftsbank (Land Credit Bank) for the next two days. This T-34/85 abandoned in front of the University Hall was hit by a Panzerfaust launched from the first floor by Leutnant Otto Geib. (Zbigniew Zielonacki)

other sectors. The Soviets realised that the German command had assigned most of their best soldiers to the east part of the city, which they considered the most vulnerable. On 25th January, Colonel Aleksey Uskov, commander of the 244th Rifle Regiment of the 82nd Guards Rifle Division, was mortally wounded by German machine-gun fire and he died two days later. In another attack on the Flak-Höhe on 27th January the defenders kept the Russian attackers at bay. However the defences were about to be denuded as one of the two batteries defending the hill was recalled to bolster the defences of the Citadel, thus weakening this position considerably.

That day a short radio message reached Festung headquarters informing them about a forthcoming attempt to relieve the besieged city. Indeed, the following day, a Kampfgruppe created from cadets of the infantry school

Schlossfreiheit had been known as Marszalka Pilsudskiego Avenue before the war, was renamed Czerwonej Armii (Red Army) Street in 1945 and then in 1989 received its current name, Swietego Marcin Street. The University Hall, a neo-Renaissance building erected in 1905-10, remains shorn of its battle damage. (Tomasz Zgoda)

in Döberitz and Sturmgeschütz-Brigade 111 attacked near the town of Benschen, 85 kilometres west of Poznan. However, they were soon stopped and with this failure the last hope for the encircled city evaporated.

The relentless gnawing away at the defences continued. On January 28th a further Soviet assault was made on Fort II on the south-eastern edge of the city. The attack reached the woodland around the fort. In confused fighting Oberfeldwebel Josef Schreiber, a winner of the Knight's Cross with Oak Leaves went missing just outside the fort's moat, never to be seen again.

The following days brought more heavy fighting on both sides of Warschauer Strasse, the main road into the city from the east. On 29th January, forces of the 117th Rifle Division managed to get on top of Fort II but, with help of the German artillery plastering their own fort, they were repulsed.

Confidence in the conduct of the fighting on the German side had reached crisis point. On the orders of Reichsführer-SS Heinrich Himmler, the commander of Heeresgruppe Weichsel, Generalmajor Mattern was removed from his post with immediate effect on 31st January. The reason for his sacking could reasonably be attributed to Mattern's incompetence as he had in effect dumped the defence of the city onto his Chief-of-Staff, Oberst Erwin Dettbarn. More likely, however, is that it was due to his relentless requests

Part I. Festung Posen • 35

A German 8.8cm PaK 43 anti-tank gun lies abandoned in front of the Imperial Castle. It was destroyed by Katyusha fire almost immediately after it had been emplaced. (Zbigniew Zielonacki)

to Himmler for orders to allow the garrison to abandon the city. Mattern's replacement was Oberst Ernst Gonell, commander of Sector East. Gonell was promoted to Generalmajor and his former post was given to Major Fritz Schulte. Generalmajor Mattern was relegated to command of a newly formed Sector Centre (Abschnitt Mitte) charged with defending the inner city.

By the beginning of February, the number of German troops manning Sector East had been reduced by half, due either to combat losses or because troops had been transferred to the more-threatened Sector Centre. Even more significant was the loss of nearly all of its artillery and assault guns either destroyed or through a lack of ammunition.

On 1st February, an infantry battalion of Moiseyevski's 312th Rifle Division, in position south of the city, successfully crossed the Warthe from west to east, coming ashore behind – and thus avoiding – the line of the forts on the east bank. After this success, the battalion advanced north

Looking back west along Swietego Marcin Street in 2019. (Tomasz Zgoda)

towards the Bamberg district. The next few days brought heavy fighting for the Luisenhain railway bridge, the nearby brickyard and the Luisenhain district. Finally, on the 4th, Moiseyevski's troops captured the railway bridge intact, gaining for the Red Army a prime opportunity to support their forces at the Oder front with railway transport. One of the main reasons for the Germans clinging onto Festung Posen was lost.

That same day, 4th February, the Flak-Höhe had to be abandoned, the Germans blowing up the last remaining guns before leaving the feature to the Soviets. On this and the following days, the Germans lost a whole series of forts on the east bank. On the 4th they left Fort Ia. That same night they abandoned Fort II, and two days later Fort IIIa was surrounded. The next day, Koberidze's 117th Rifle Division started a fresh attack along Warschauer Strasse and on 8th February, Forts IIa, III and IIIa fell. By the 9th, constant attacks by the 312th Rifle Division had pushed the Germans north towards Fort Rauch, the older fort located just south-east of the Altstadt. The Soviets slowly battled their way forward for another week.

By this time, half of Sector East was in Russian hands. The new German defence line ran from Wallischei on the eastern side of the Altstadt along the Warthe to Fort Radziwill, then south of the Dom-Insel (cathedral island), and from there along the Cybina river to the western part of the Heinrichstadt district. Around this time Major Schulte, the commander of Sector East,

Part I. Festung Posen • 37

A 152mm SU-152 assault gun of the 394th Guards Heavy Assault Gun Regiment was disabled on Kurfürsten-Ring (Waly Zygmunta Starego), the avenue leading south-east from the Schlossfreiheit. The SU-152 was a powerful weapon and because of its ability to knock out the heaviest German armoured vehicles – including Tiger and Panther tanks – it gained the nickname Zveroboy ('Beast Slayer'). (Zbigniew Zielonacki)

The same SU-152 can be seen in the background of this still from combat footage taken by a Red Army cameraman. Two German soldiers have emerged from the building on the right and surrender to the Russians. This was in the sector of the 240th Rifle Regiment of the 74th Guards Rifle Division. (Soviet Newsreel)

Waly Zygmunta Starego is today Niepodleglosci (Independence) Avenue and the building at No. 8 has been splendidly restored. (Tomasz Zgoda)

suffered a minor concussion from a Soviet artillery strike and was replaced by Major Hahn, previously in command of Sector Warthe.

The last remaining defenders of Fort Rauch hastily withdrew to the Dom-Insel on 11th February after most of the fort had been demolished by constant Soviet shelling. Two days later the 117th Rifle Division finally managed to secure the Heinrichstadt district albeit after a very long and bitter fight.

On the night of 13th/14th February, the crew of Fort I, the last bastion still holding out in the south-east, was forced to break out in an attempt to reach the German lines to the west. This decision was taken because all previous efforts to fight their way out towards the forces still holding out in the city, to the north, had failed. Only a few of them eventually managed to reach the Neisse river near the town of Forst, thus escaping certain Soviet captivity.

On 14th February, the Germans tried to blow up the Gerber-Damm railway bridge, which crossed the Warthe just south-east of the Citadel. The attempt was only partially successful, probably due to the poor quality of the explosives at hand. This day also saw another attempt by the 117th Rifle Division to overcome the German resistance in this sector, particularly along Warschauer Strasse, at the Bahnhof Posen Ost and at the Deutsche

Part I. Festung Posen • 39

This T-34/85 from the 250th Independent Tank Regiment was knocked out on Martin-Strasse as it penetrated deeper into the Old Town from Schlossfreiheit. This stretch of the street lay on the boundary between the 27th and 74th Guards Rifle Divisions so it is difficult to say which formation it was supporting.

Swietego Marcin is nowadays one of the busiest streets in Poznan. This is its crossing with Ratajczaka Street (Ritter-Strasse). Although the houses here survived the fighting, this is not true of the whole street as the entire northern side of Swietego Marcin behind the photographer was destroyed and has since been redeveloped. (Tomasz Zgoda)

Munitions-Werke (DMW) ordnance factory. They were all repulsed but it was the last straw for the Germans.

15th February was the last day of organised defence in Sector East. The 117th Rifle Division along with the 312th Rifle Division managed to break into the Oststadt district, the DMW factory and the firing range north of the Cybina river. A complete collapse of the whole defence of this sector was only delayed by the use of Kompanie Nölke in the DMW factory and Kompanie Tiegel in the area of the firing range. In the afternoon Generalmajor Gonell ordered all those in the sector who could still carry arms to break out of the surrounded city and try to reach friendly lines in Pomerania. Around 1,000 soldiers, half of them wounded, gathered in the Oststadt district south-west of Fort IV intending to attempt the escape. A rear-guard was to cover the escape effort, which was made on the 16th. Having seen them off, the rear guard was to then withdraw towards the Citadel. The Russians soon followed up. With no forces left to oppose them, the 117th and 312th Rifle Divisions advanced and captured the abandoned Fort IV and the old Forts Radziwill, Prittwitz and Rauch.

T-34/76 tanks supporting the 240th Rifle Regiment grind their way through the rubble on Alter Markt (Stary Rynek), the Old Market Square. They are moving eastwards into Breite Strasse (Wielka Street). (RGAKFiD)

Completely rebuilt, although mostly in a different architectural style, Stary Rynek is again the vibrant heart of the city and a magnet for tourists. (Tomasz Zgoda)

At a certain point in the battle, the Tiger of the Panzer-Stoss-Reserve – the single tank of this type in the detachment – made a surprise sally from Nieder-Wall (Kosciuszki Street), a side street of Martin-Strasse, and with its powerful 88mm gun knocked out four IS-2 tanks from the 11th Guards Heavy Tank Regiment, which were stationary in Tiergarten-Strasse (Marszalka Pilsudskiego Avenue) on the far side of the Schloss-Brücke. Here two of the tanks are seen after the fighting. The view is eastwards across the Schloss-Brücke, towards the spot from where the Tiger opened fire. Just across the bridge, on the left, is the University Hall with the tower of the Imperial Castle protruding above it. It appears that engineers from a Soviet tank maintenance unit have removed the tracks and bogie wheels from the right-hand tank. (Zbigniew Zielonacki)

FIGHTING FOR THE OLD TOWN

31st January to 17th February

By the end of January, Glebov's 27th Guards Rifle Division had reached the area of the main railway line running through the city along the eastern side of the Hermannstadt district. To its right, Bakanov's 74th Guards Rifle Division slowly pushed forward in the area of Fort Grolman and north of Burggrafen-Ring. On 2nd February, Marchenko's 39th Guards Rifle Division

The part of Marszalka Pilsudskiego Avenue that lay west of the Old City was named Zwierzyniecka Street after the war. Its crossing with Roosevelta Street was turned into a major roundabout known as the **Rondo Kaponiera.** (Tomasz Zgoda)

Part I. Festung Posen • 43

The same tank seen from the other side. Note the damage to the building across the street. (Zbigniew Zielonacki)

The ruined houses were pulled down after the war, the site now having being redeveloped for the Mercury Hotel. (Tomasz Zgoda)

pushed the Germans out of the Jersitz district towards the city centre. The Soviet offensive stopped there as the Germans established a solid defence line along the substantial buildings of the city centre, which they had named Abschnitt Mitte. The line of public buildings was crucial to block access to this part of the city.

In the last days of January, troops of the 27th Guards Rifle Division penetrated into the Altstadt from the west via the Schloss-Brücke and captured the assembly hall of the Reichs-Universität Posen located nearby. Fierce combat raged in this area for several days. During one of these fights another holder of the Knight's Cross, Oberfeldwebel Gerhard Scholz was killed.

The crew of a Russian 122mm M1938 (M-30) howitzer, emplaced at the north-east corner of Alter Markt (Stary Rynek), the city's Old Town Market, takes aim at the enemy entrenched in Breite Strasse (Wielka Street).

Breite Strasse has today become Wielka Street.
(Tomasz Zgoda)

Prowling the area around the university was the lone Tiger I tank from the Panzer-Stoss-Reserve. During one of its forays it knocked out four IS-2 tanks that had taken up position on the west side of the Schloss-Brücke.

A number of the Soviet commanders had learned the lessons of street-fighting from fighting the Wehrmacht in battles such as Stalingrad. They quickly organised special assault groups to storm the Altstadt consisting

Part I. Festung Posen • 45

A Studebaker 6 x 6 truck, provided to the Soviet Union under the Lend-Lease programme, and towing a 122mm M1938 (M-30) howitzer, passes in front of the Town Hall on the Alter Markt. Although it is not evident in this image, the Town Hall was badly damaged in the fighting, losing its tower completely. (RGAKFiD)

The 16th-century Renaissance building was painstakingly restored in 1945-54, and today houses the Museum of the History of Poznan on Stary Rynek. (Tomasz Zgoda)

of small infantry teams equipped with flame-throwers and explosives, supported by artillery pieces and tanks. The first to form such groups as early as 31st January, was the 74th Guards Rifle Division. The close co-operation of different arms proved to be very effective in urban warfare.

The 27th Guards Rifle Division managed to capture the university buildings on 1st February and in so doing, prevented the Germans from

The crew of a ZIS-3 anti-tank gun takes a break in the small courtyard of a housing block along Fremden-Gasse (Zydowska Alley), one of the streets leading north from the Old Market. Note that the gun on the left is covered with a Wehrmacht Zeltbahn (a combined rain smock and tent section). (RGAKFiD)

This part of the Old Town used to be the centre of the Jewish quarter of Poznan but by 1945 there were no Jews remaining, as all 2,000 of them had been deported to the Generalgouvernement as a first step towards their mass murder in the Nazi death camps. Zydowska Street literally translates as Jews Alley and it is telling of the Nazi policy to expunge anything Jewish that they would rename it Fremden-Gasse (Foreigners Alley) instead. Today, a plaque on a wall in the courtyard at Nos. 15-18 commemorates the Jewish citizens of Poznan who lost their lives during the Nazi occupation. (Tomasz Zgoda)

leaving them. Almost all of the defenders were either killed or taken prisoner during escape attempts. The Soviets also captured the Faculty of Medical Sciences building and the southern part of the Jersitz district. They then broke into the Schlossfreiheit, once the Imperial palace and more recently Gauleiter Greiser's former residence. By this point in the battle the building had been turned into a military hospital with some 1,500 to 2,000 wounded. Confusion on the German side was such that no one even thought about evacuating them.

The Schlossfreiheit fell fully into Soviet hands on the following day along with the Economic Faculty and the Railways Management building on Nieder-Wall. The attackers stormed in past the palace and along the broad Martin-Strasse but were soon stopped by the defenders on the barricade at its crossing with Bismarck-Strasse. The close fighting in the inner city prompted the troops of the 27th Guards Rifle Division into adopting the assault groups tactics already employed by 74th Guards Rifle Division.

Under relentless attack, the Germans were forced to abandon the area around Fort Grolman on 3rd February. They organised a new defensive line further north in the area of the city gasworks and power plant, and also manned two small bridgeheads on the west bank of the Warthe at the Sankt-Rochus-Brücke and the Wallischei-Brücke. The Red Army forces were now advancing towards the Citadel from both south and west. Separate battles were waged for the German outposts holding out in the Altstadt, the fighting at its fiercest around the bridges and the river harbour just north of the gasworks.

Between the 27th and 74th Guards Rifle Divisions lay yet another Deutsche Munitions-Werke ordnance factory. They were also separated by the stretch of railway tracks south of the main railway station and the station building itself – all of them still in German hands – preventing coordination between the two divisions. In order to rectify this problem an assault was launched on the area, which resulted in the capture of the station on 3rd February, and of the DMW factory two days later.

On 6th February the Sankt-Rochus-Brücke, the southernmost road bridge over the Warthe, was blown up and subsequently set alight. The northern span, the Wallischei-Brücke, was blown for a second time on the 9th but it remained passable for foot soldiers. The heavy combat for the Altstadt finally ended on 11th February. By then 60 per cent of the historical buildings, among them the Town Hall, lay in ruins.

After taking the Altstadt the Citadel lay only around 500 metres away to the north. However, lying between the Soviet forces and the fortress was an area of densely packed streets composed of a myriad of partially ruined buildings. Fighting through this rabbit warren lasted until 16th February before the obstacle was finally overcome. The way to the Citadel from the south side now lay open.

Attempts to penetrate the enemy positions were also made from the west. The German line here ran along the railway embankment, which at this point curved from south to east. After the Soviets pierced this line, they pushed forward through the Goethe-Park, and along Dietrich-Eckart-Strasse and the Herse-Wall. More to the right, pushing along Leo-Schlageter-Strasse and Berliner Strasse, they got towards Wilhelm-Platz. All of the bridges along the railway embankment were blown up on 6th February to prevent the Red Army from using them to cut off the remaining defenders of the Altstadt from the Citadel.

The chief remaining zones of German resistance were the barracks located on Magazin-Strasse along with a number of nearby buildings. The battle for

A wrecked SU-152 assault gun lies on the west bank of the Warthe river at the Chwaliszewski Bridge (Wallischei-Brücke). It arrived here while supporting the 236th Rifle Regiment of the 74th Guards Rifle Division in their attacks on the German position maintained around this bridge, and was knocked out with a Panzerfaust by Fahnenjunker-Unteroffizier Paul Jasper on 7th February. Two days later, Jasper again showed great courage when he blew up the bridge in an attempt to deny it to the Russians. However, the demolished span could still be crossed by infantry, and six days later the Russians managed to get across and gain a foothold on the Dom Insel (Cathedral Island), allowing them to subdue the last resistance in this quarter of the city. (Zbigniew Zielonacki)

The Chwaliszewski Bridge crossed the Warthe at a point where it curved towards the Old Town. Since the war, the river has been straightened and today the site of the former bridge is where Wielka Street becomes Chwaliszewo Street. The new Warthe bridge is a few hundred metres further on.

Part I. Festung Posen • 49

During the course of the fighting, every one of the eighteen forts ringing the city (all being named after Prussian generals), fell or were abandoned by their garrisons which usually comprised a company of infantry. Fort Va, also known as Fort Bonin, was situated north of the city, and was doggedly held by a company of troops under a Leutnant. One of the last forts to be captured, it finally fell after a heavy artillery barrage followed by a massed attack by the 82nd Guards Rifle Division on 16th February. (MWN/A. Dugaron)

Although now abandoned and overgrown with trees, Fort Va remains basically intact. Damage from the Russian shelling can still be seen. The word 'Zwischenwerk' in the title above the gate indicates that it was one of the intermediary forts, which is also indicated by the suffix 'a' to its Roman numeral. (Tomasz Zgoda)

this area and for the two streets leading north on either side of it, the Kaiser-Ring and Adalbert-Strasse, lasted nine days, from 9th to 17th February. The struggle to capture the Sankt-Adalbert-Kirche, at the northern end of the Adalbert-Strasse, started on 9th February. Soviet records state it was taken on the 10th but according to German sources it was not taken until the 15th. Over the following days the nearby cemetery fell into Russian hands. Finally, the starting point for an assault on the Citadel was secured.

Glebov's 27th Guards Rifle Division handed over its positions south-east of the Citadel to Bakanov's 74th Guards Rifle Division on 12th February, and moved north to relieve Khetagurov's 82nd Guards Rifle Division, which in turn shifted to positions south-west of the Citadel.

STORMING THE CITADEL

18th to 23rd February

By 17th February all of the German forces remaining in Festung Posen were crammed into the area of the Citadel and its neighbourhood. An estimated 4,000 soldiers, many of them wounded and exhausted, found shelter within its walls. Only around half of them were still able to fight and these were divided into four combat groups:

- Kampfgruppe Beisser, (Oberleutnant Heinrich Beisser) holding the northern left flank,
- Kampfgruppe Werner, (Hauptmann Fritz Werner) holding the northern right flank,
- Kampfgruppe Hohlfeld, (Major Karl Hohlfeld) defending the southern right flank,
- Kampfgruppe Ewert, (Major Heinz Martin Ewert) manning the southern left flank.

In addition to infantry, the force comprised a couple of armoured vehicles and a few guns in the Citadel. However, most of the heavy weapons had dwindling stocks of ammunition.

The situation of the defenders was critical. They suffered not only from the heavy Soviet artillery and aerial bombardment but also from a lack of water. Their water supply had been cut off by a group of Polish civilians acting on their own initiative. Both food and alcohol were plentiful, the fort's storerooms holding abundant supplies. However, the care of the wounded was on the point of collapse. Lacking any central facility, they were dispersed across a number of casemates and rooms within the Citadel, making coherent care next to impossible as movement them from one part of the fort to another was only practical after dark. Medical supplies had become scarce, which made their sorry plight even worse.

Meanwhile, the Soviets were preparing for the final assault. As the terrain on the northern side of the Citadel favoured the defence, the attack was to be made from the south. Here the terrain gradually sloped up towards the fort. Khetagurov's 82nd Guards Rifle Division were to come in from the south-

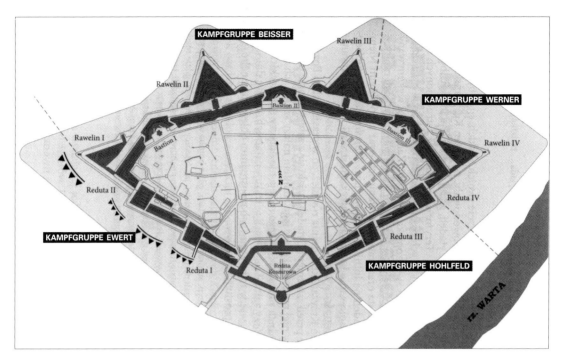

By 17th February, all of Poznan had been captured except for the last German bastion, the Citadel, or Kernwerk as the Germans called it, located on the hill north of the Old Town. Built in 1828-42, it comprised a fortified main barracks on the southern (city) side, flanked by four redoubts, with ravelins (detached outworks) at either end. On the northern side were three bastions with two more ravelins, and the entire fort was surrounded by a deep dry moat. Here the last German defenders, some 4,000 of them, half of them wounded, entrenched themselves for the final battle. (Maciej Karalus)

west and Bakanov's 74th Guards Rifle Division from the south-east. Glebov's 27th Guards Rifle Division was tasked with blocking off the Citadel from the north. The attack would be supported by numerous artillery units fielding a total of 236 guns and mortars, including heavy 203mm and 280mm pieces.

During the evening, General Chuikov, the 8th Guards Army commander, sent two captured German officers as envoys to the Citadel, hoping they could convince the German command to surrender. However, Generalmajor Gonell and his staff refused the offer, deciding to fight on.

At 0700-hrs on 18th February, the Soviet artillery opened fire on the German positions on the southern side of the Citadel. The barrage crashed down on the beleaguered force for four hours. The shellfire was directed primarily at field positions on top of the fortifications, its embrasures, and the fort's main redoubt. In order to deceive the defenders about the direction of the planned attack, the guns also plastered the northern part of the Citadel. Close-support aircraft from the 16th Air Army contributed their share, bombing and strafing the fort. When the artillery fire had opened up, the German troops had taken whatever shelter they could find but, as soon as the guns fell silent, they flooded back to their positions.

The assault force stormed forward at 1100-hrs. The soldiers of the 82nd Guards Rifle Division had to cross open terrain before reaching the slopes of the Citadel, taking casualties all the way. All day Khetagurov's men tried to root the defenders out of their trenches and gun positions but the men

The assault on the Citadel started on 18th February but for the first two days the German lines held, a small penetration on the first night being thrown back the following morning. However, on the 20th, troops of the 246th Rifle Regiment of the 82nd Guards Rifle Division gained a toehold inside the fort and during the night managed to build a wooden bridge over the moat near Redoubt II, permitting more infantry, and anti-tank guns, to enter the fortress. Here Captain Shetiel Abramov, the commander of the 3rd Assault Group of the 246th Rifle Regiment, and some his men proudly pose on the bridge after the battle.
(MWN/A. Dugaron)

In 1963-70 most of the fortifications of the Citadel were demolished and nearly all of the moat filled in, and the whole area was developed into what became the city's Park Cytadela, today a popular public meeting place. Although completely changed, this is the spot where the makeshift bridge was built.
(Tomasz Zgoda)

of Kampfgruppe Ewert held their ground. Meanwhile, on the right, the 74th Guards Rifle Division battled all day to force their way into the Gerber-Damm Railway Station and a complex of military buildings at the foot of the slope. They too had no success.

However, during the night soldiers of the 82nd Guards Rifle Division finally managed to force a path across the Citadel's moat at Redoubt I. Clawing out a foothold on the other side, they immediately began construction of

Part I. Festung Posen • 53

Faced with an acute manpower shortage, Major-General Afanasi Shemenkov, the commander of the 29th Guards Rifle Corps, ordered Nikolai Smirnov, the Soviet Military Commander of Poznan, to organise a mobilisation of Polish civilians. After consultation with the newly-appointed governor of Wielkopolska province (and plenipotentiary of the Moscow-appointed Provisional Polish Government), Michal Gwiazdovicz, and the new Mayor of Poznan, Feliks Maciejewski (he had been appointed by Gwiazdovicz on 9th February), Smirnov announced conscription. Voluntary and forced recruitment brought in some 2,000 men. They were tasked with keeping order in the city and some 500 also took part in the fighting for the Citadel. A Soviet combat cameraman filmed some of the militiamen leaving their headquarters at No. 57 Dr.-Wilms-Strasse (Matejki Street) in the Hermannstadt (Górczyn) district. The building next-door, No. 59, had earlier been the local headquarters of the underground Polska Partia Robotnicza (Polish Worker Party). (Polish Newsreel Kronika Filmowa)

It remains little changed and today houses a municipal housing agency. (Tomasz Zgoda)

a makeshift bridge in order that they could span the moat. As the light of dawn revealed their work the Germans realised what was happening. In a desperate attempt at self-preservation, they managed to destroy the nascent span, throwing the Russian troops back across the moat to the southern slopes. The new day did not improve matters for the Russians. On the contrary, in the course of the day's fighting the 82nd Guards Rifle Division lost Major Boris Belyayev and Captain Fiodor Sarichev, both later awarded Hero of the Soviet Union medals.

The following day, the 20th, the artillery bombardment resumed at 0630-hrs. It reached its crescendo at 0830-hrs with salvos of fire from Katyusha rocket launchers, raining projectiles down on the slowly diminishing German force. By this time, the Soviet shelling and air bombardment had forced the defenders from the slopes of the citadel, forcing them to seek shelter in its subterranean vaults. Ammunition for heavy weapons was exhausted and the garrison were only able to continue their resistance by firing from the fort's embrasures. At 1100-hrs soldiers of the 82nd Guards Rifle Division were once again able to cross the moat and this time it was possible to plant two red flags on the Citadel's ramparts. Looking for a place to build a crossing over the moat, they selected the area of Redoubt II at the western end of the fortress – the moat was shallower there and the distance from the main redoubt was greater, thus making German harassing fire less effective. At 2000-hrs a makeshift bridge for infantry was begun. In order to shield the construction from German fire a pile of wood, debris and other materials had been dumped to provide cover. Meanwhile, on the right, the 74th Guards Rifle Division finally managed to break through to the railway running directly in front of the Citadel.

Redoubt II was attacked with explosive charges being dropped into the ventilation shaft. This detonated the artillery shells stored inside, resulting in a massive explosion that killed and wounded many of the defenders, leaving them no choice but to surrender. Here, after the battle, the conquerors stand outside the entrance to the redoubt. (MWN/A. Dugaron)

Today, only some vestiges of Redoubt II remain – one of the very few visible relics of the battle in the present-day park. (Tomasz Zgoda)

Both attacking divisions were by now understrength depleted, as they were, after a month of heavy fighting in the city. To support their efforts the Soviets announced the mobilisation of Polish citizens. The Poles were not told why they were being mobilised nor where they would be deployed, though the opportunity to get even with the Germans after five and a half years of occupation may have motivated some. However most felt coerced into joining up because of the threat of penalty were they not to comply. Some 2,000 Poles came forward and were employed in and around the citadel, usually operating in small groups. One of these was sent to help with building the bridge over the moat near Redoubt II, and another was armed with rifles and grenades and supported the 74th Guards Rifle Division in capturing the main redoubt.

Early on the morning of 21st February, the 82nd Guards engineers and their Polish helpers finished the improvised bridge over the moat. This

Part I. Festung Posen • 55

The Citadel's fortified main barracks was severely pummelled by multiple Soviet artillery barrages and bomber attacks. This is how it looked after the battle. In the foreground lies the wreck of a SdKfz 4 Maultier half-track.
(MWN/A. Dugaron)

enabled them to reinforce the group already on the Citadel with a large force of troops and to bring over anti-tank guns. In order to flush the Germans out of Redoubt II, they dropped explosives into the ventilation shafts. The explosions ignited an ammunition store within, which detonated violently in a series of explosions. Many of the 180 wounded in the underground rooms were killed or wounded anew by the blasts. After 20 minutes of continual fire and explosions, the German troops manning the position surrendered. Soon the adjoining Ravelin I, on the western corner of the Citadel, was also under attack. A group of around 30 Germans had been defending with around 240 wounded men sheltering inside. They put up a tough resistance and withstood all attacks, even though the Russians tried to force them to surrender with flame-throwers and explosive charges thrown into the embrasures.

Meanwhile, on the right flank, soldiers of the 74th Guards Rifle Division and their Polish reinforcements were storming the Citadel's main redoubt. After the artillery had pushed the German defenders back from the embrasures, they filled the moat in front of the main gate and dragged an anti-tank gun into position. With the help of this gun, they were able to hold the ground gained inside the fortress. However, the Germans were still blocking access to the fort's main square.

A third Soviet division then joined the fray. Glebov's 27th Guards Rifle Division arrived, having been relieved in the north by Koberidze's 117th Rifle Division. It was tasked with storming the Citadel from the south-west.

Defending the position north of the Citadel throughout this battle was the lone Tiger I. Fighting on in spite of being immobilised, it managed to destroy a total of ten Soviet tanks and other vehicles during the last days of the battle.

In order to get at the barracks' northern block, the troops of the 74th Guards Rifle Division had to charge across a 100-metre-wide courtyard, an impossible task against the German machine gunners entrenched in the building. This view is looking south, across to the Citadel's main gate and the Russian positions. The 3rd Battalion of the 236th Rifle Regiment was to the right of the gate and the 1st Battalion of the 226th Rifle Regiment to the left. (Stanislaw Poradowski)

Absolutely nothing remains standing of the barracks today and there is now simply just parkland and trees where battle raged over 75 years ago. (Tomasz Zgoda)

Generalmajor Gonell received word via the Festung staff that he had been awarded the Knight's Cross on 21st February. Gonell ordered that the award be kept a secret in order to avoid irritating the soldiers of his dwindling command.

The fifth day of the battle for the Citadel started with the usual artillery barrage commencing at 0630-hrs – this time 90 minutes long – after which the Soviet troops renewed their efforts to break the German resistance. All day, they tried to cross the 100-metre-wide courtyard to the main redoubt's northern barrack block but all attempts faltered in front of withering fire from the German machine-guns. With the end clearly in sight, the German

Part I. Festung Posen • 57

All through the battle for the Citadel, the lone Tiger tank from the Panzer-Stoss-Reserve fought off all Russian attacks directed at the fortress from the north. In early February, after several engagements in the Old Town, the tank had been withdrawn to the Citadel to repair its damaged gun sight. When a Katyusha barrage threatened to destroy it, one of the assistant crewmen, Obergefreiter Fischer, courageously drove it out of the field of fire. However, he did not know how to properly use the gearbox and ruined the clutch, thus immobilising the tank. A Sturmgeschütz later towed it out of the fort to a position on Steuben-Allee (Za Cytadela Street), the road curving along the fortress's northern side, from where it had a good field of fire towards the Zeppelinwiese. In the following days the tank, crewed by Unteroffizier Fred Heckmann (originally its loader but now its commander), Obergefreiter Richard Siegert (gun aimer) and Gefreiter Kurt Algner (loader, replaced by Obergefreiter Everoth when Algner was seriously wounded), destroyed five T-34s, three artillery tractors towing one 203mm heavy howitzer, two IS-2 tanks and one 76mm anti-tank gun. This is a still lifted from Russian footage taken at the end of the fighting. The house seen in the background was used by the tank crew as a shelter.

Neatly repaired, the house at No. 96 Za Cytadela Street still stands.
(Tomasz Zgoda)

58 • RED ARMY TOWARDS THE ODER – THEN AND NOW

In addition to the Tiger, two Panthers, a Hetzer and several StuG assault guns, the Panzer-Stoss-Reserve had a Panzer IV and one StuH 42 assault howitzer. Both were found inside the Citadel after the battle.
(Comparison from Tomasz Zgoda)

command sent its very last radio communication which stated that the Festung was expected to fall on the next day. The same conclusion was also obvious to General Chuikov who once again sent two captured German officers as truce envoys. Again, Gonell refused to surrender.

In the early hours of 23rd February, a large group of soldiers from Kampfgruppe Beisser tried to break out through the lines of the 117th Rifle Division. However, few of them made it, most of them falling victim to Soviet shells and small-arms fire. Meanwhile the final assault on the main

The bridge over the moat at the Citadel's northern gate. It was here that large groups of German soldiers tried to break out from the fort during the night of 22nd/23rd February, a first attempt being made shortly after midnight and a second a few hours later shortly after dawn. However, very few of the escapees made it to friendly lines. (MWN/A. Dugaron)

Today, only a small section of the bridge is still visible, the larger part having been buried. (Tomasz Zgoda)

redoubt was taking place. This time German resistance were less resilient. Even small arms ammunition was running out and this enabled the Soviets and Poles finally to overcome this part of the Citadel. Engineers of the 82nd Guards Rifle Division blew up part of the moat wall between Ravelin I and Redoubt I in order to prepare a ramp into the fort so that armoured vehicles could be committed to the final crushing of opposition.

At around 0600-hrs another group of around 500 German soldiers made a final desperate bid to break out of the Citadel from Ravelin III on the fortress's northern side. Fewer than half their number survived the attempt. The events of that morning demonstrated that no more could be done and Generalmajor Gonell was forced to capitulate, even though orders from Himmler expressly forbade him to do so. His overriding concern was for the

On 23rd February, the day the Citadel was captured, the Soviets lined up a series of ZIS-3 guns in front of the Imperial Castle to fire a salute to celebrate their victory. At that moment, the castle was being used as a PoW cage for German prisoners. (MWN/A. Dugaron)

Fully renovated, the Imperial Castle, or Zamek Cesarski in Polish, is today a centre of culture, housing art galleries, a cinema, a puppet theatre and music clubs. Its courtyard is a venue for open-air concerts and movie screenings during summer. (Tomasz Zgoda)

wounded, over 2,000 of whom were still trapped in the Citadel. He sent two of his staff officers – his chief Flak officer, Major Erich Kurth, and his chief doctor, Oberstabsarzt Dr Heinrich Geuder – to General Chuikov as parleys. After a short talk with the commander of the 8th Guards Army, they returned to the Citadel. The fight was over. German soldiers started to surrender, emerging from the subterranean hell in which they had been sheltering.

Part I. Festung Posen • 61

A few days later, the Soviets marched a large number of German prisoners through the city – a propaganda exercise staged for the benefit of the local population as well as the Russian war correspondents and photographers. It was also reminiscent of the massive PoW marches organised in Leningrad and Moscow earlier in the war. This photo was taken on Kurfürsten-Ring (Waly Zygmunta Starego), the wide avenue leading south from Schlossfreiheit. On the right is the Landgenossenschaftsbank (Land Credit Bank), a heavily-contested building during the fighting in early February.

Both the Imperial Castle and the bank building, now the Poznan Philharmonic, have lost part of their towers in the post-war restoration. The street is now Niepodleglosci Avenue. (Tomasz Zgoda)

62 • RED ARMY TOWARDS THE ODER – THEN AND NOW

The Soviet troops showed no mercy towards the German non-walking wounded captured in the Citadel, most of them being shot or burned to death with flame-throwers. Here Russian soldiers watch some of the unfortunates burning alive in the shed located between the embankments of Redoubt II. In the background is the western block of the main barracks. (MWN/A. Dugaron)

It difficult to pinpoint precisely where the shed stood in the present-day park but this is its approximate position. (Tomasz Zgoda)

However, not all were willing to accept the capitulation to the Soviets. Generalmajor Gonell committed suicide, shooting himself with a pistol just as his emissaries arrived back with the first Russians. The same choice was made by SS-Standartenführer Rudolf Lange, commander of Gestapo in Posen, along with a number of other officers and men. Generalmajor Mattern was taken prisoner.

Part I. Festung Posen • 63

As soon as the Soviets had captured the Schlossfreiheit in early February, they began using the area between the University Hall and the Imperial Palace as a burial ground for their fallen soldiers. These interments continued until the end of the battle, with Polish civilians attending the ceremonies – on many days in great numbers. The building across the street on the left is the State Academy of Music, another heavily-scarred building during the fighting in early February. MWN/A. Dugaron)

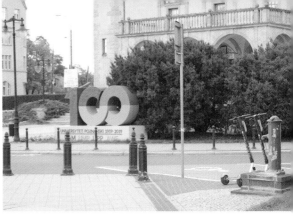

It was only a temporary burial ground, all the dead being later exhumed and transferred to the Soviet War Cemetery established on the south-western slope of Citadel hill. Today there are no graves left on Adam Mickiewicz Square. The music school is now known as the Ignacy Jan Paderewski Academy of Music, named after the Polish composer, diplomat and politician (1860-1941). (Tomasz Zgoda)

The University Hall still houses the directorate of Poznan University, which celebrated its centenary in 2019. (Tomasz Zgoda)

THE COST

The reduction of Festung Posen had been a costly battle for both sides. The exact number of German dead is not known. An estimated 4,000 to 5,000 of them fell in battle but added to that must be several hundreds of captured wounded who, unable to move, were shot or burned alive with flame-throwers by the Russians. In addition, many of those who were taken prisoner died later in temporary POW camps in the city, on their way to the USSR or because of forced labour while they were there. Only a few of those who managed to break out of the Festung were lucky enough to reach friendly lines.

Soviet combat losses were slightly higher than the German, amounting to around 5,500 killed or wounded, though many who survived were then sent on to take part in the final assault on Germany.

Casualties among the Polish inhabitants of the city were also heavy. An estimated 600 Polish civilians were killed during the fighting and from the 2,000 militiamen that helped the Russians in taking the Citadel, around 100 are understood to have perished.

The Soviet War Cemetery contains the graves of 3,678 Red Army soldiers. Nearby is a Commonwealth cemetery – Poznan Old Garrison Cemetery – set up after the First World War and containing 457 graves, mostly of British POWs from that war and airmen from the Second War, including those who lost their lives in the Great Escape. Both cemeteries are overlooked by a 'Heroes' Monument' which stands at the top of the flight of steps that forms the main entrance to the park. (Tomasz Zgoda)

PART II.
DEFENDING THE ODER

The Landkreis (rural district) of Königsberg-in-der-Neumark was, until 1945, a canton of the province of Brandenburg in Prussia. The canton's administrative centre Königsberg (today Chojna in Poland), located some 80 kilometres north-east of Berlin and about equidistant from the pre-war German/Polish frontier, was a small country town of some 6,700 inhabitants. The surrounding district, lying immediately east of the Oder river, was for the larger part of the war, one of the most-peaceful areas of Nazi Germany. The absence of any industry that could be a target of the Allied bombing campaign and the remoteness of the fighting fronts allowed the civilian population to feel quite safe.

Schwedt is a small town on the west bank of the Oder. Dating back to the 13th century and featuring a large castle, a hospital and several military barracks, in 1945 it had a population of some 9,000. The River Oder in this area is lined by the Friedrichsthal Canal, which runs parallel to the river on its western side, the three-kilometre-wide strip in between being swampy marshland. The road running east out of Schwedt across the swampland crossed a series of six bridges, the two main ones being a long steel bridge over the canal just outside the town and a five-span bridge over the main course of the Oder river just before it reaches the village of Nieder-Kränig (today Krajnik Dolny in Poland) on the east bank.

THE SCHWEDT BRIDGEHEAD

The first orders to create a bridgehead east of Schwedt were given on 27th January 1945. In the chaos of the retreating German armies the intention was to establish a defensive line along which they might stop the Russian advance. However, the orders could not be implemented immediately due to a lack of available troops. Notwithstanding the obstacles involved, three bridgeheads were somehow established along the River Oder: at Schwedt, Zehden and Zäckerick. These positions served a dual task: to defend the Oder – the last major obstacle before Berlin – and to provide a springboard for an optimistically planned counter-attack.

SKORZENY

In the early evening of 30th January, SS-Obersturmbannführer Otto Skorzeny – Hitler's favourite commando officer – was working in his office in Friedenthal Castle, twenty kilometres north of Berlin. Skorzeny is best known for having rescued Benito Mussolini, the Italian Duce, from captivity on the mountain-top resort of Gran Sasso in September 1943 – though his role was exaggerated by German propaganda. He was also noted for his covert operations behind enemy lines during the Ardennes counter-offensive in December 1944. Skorzeny was busy writing a report when his phone started ringing. On the line was

Schwedt in 1945 was a town of 9,000 people with a castle and several military barracks, it being the peacetime garrison town of Kavallerie-Regiment 6, Grenadier-Regiment Schwedt, Pionier-Bataillone 12, 32 and 42, and many other smaller units. In late January 1945, Soviet forces fell on the bridgeheads at Schwedt and Zehden. Both bridgeheads were defended by a hotchpotch of improvised and rapidly thrown together units, the one at Schwedt being defended by a formation known as Division Schwedt – commanded by Hitler's favourite commando officer, SS-Obersturmbannführer Otto Skorzeny, and the one at Zehden by the recently-formed 1. Marine-Division. Fighting on home soil, the Germans fought back tenaciously, even achieving a few local successes against the Red Army forces.

Reichsführer-SS Heinrich Himmler. Skorzeny was ordered to move 'at once', and with every soldier he could muster, to Schwedt and establish a bridgehead east of the river.

The only troops immediately available to Skorzeny were his own SS special forces units, most notably the SS-Jagdverbände and SS-Fallschirmjäger-Bataillon 600.

In late 1944, Skorzeny's disparate bands of commando troops had been organised into five so-called Jagdverbände (hunter groups). These were battalion-sized units, each named after the region of Europe where they were to be deployed (SS-Jagdverband Mitte, Ost, Südost, Südwest and Nordwest). Since the spring of 1943 the home base of the SS-Jagdverbände had been SS-Sondereinsatz-Abteilung z.b.V., Friededenthal[5]. The only units immediately at hand when Himmler's call came in were SS-Jagdverband Mitte under SS-Hauptsturmführer Karl Fucker, and one composite company from SS-Jagdverband Nordwest under SS-Hauptsturmführer Heinrich Hoyer. Hoyer's unit was theoretically made up of three kompanien, each

[5]. SS special operations unit.

Part II. Defending the Oder • 67

drawn from personnel of a particular region: 1. Kompanie was made up of Danes, Norwegians and Swedes; 2. Kompanie of Flemish; and 3. Kompanie of Dutch troops. However all three were at such low strength that they were combined into a composite company and put under command of Jagdverband Mitte.) Combined strength of the two Jagdverbände was about 680 men.

SS-Fallschirmjäger-Bataillon 600 was the only parachute unit in the Waffen-SS. It had been formed in September 1943, and originally known as Fallschirmjäger-Bataillon 500. Its first deployment was on anti-Partisan operations in Yugoslavia and its most notable activity had been Operation 'Rösselsprung', the surprise raid on Marshal Tito's headquarters in Drvar in May 1944. Since June 1944 the bataillon had been commanded by SS-Sturmbannführer Siegfried Milius. From 1st October the unit had been renumbered from 500 to 600 and on 10th November it was incorporated into the SS-Jagdverbände under Skorzeny's overall command. The bataillon participated in the Ardennes offensive as part of Skorzeny's Panzerbrigade 150 together with elements of the SS-Jagdverbände. However, by late January the battalion had returned to its barracks at Neustrelitz. With 689 men, it was at full strength and fully equipped with modern arms, including Sturmgewehre assault rifles, machine guns and LG40 7.5cm light artillery guns. It also had its own transport.

Skorzeny had access to the SS-Sturm-Kompanie, an armoured reconnaissance unit equipped with armoured cars and half-tracks under SS-Obersturmführer Otto Schwerdt; the SS-Scharfschützen-Zug, a sniper platoon of 40 men under SS-Untersturmführer Odo Wilscher; and the schwere SS-Infanterie-Geschütz-Kompanie – a battery-sized unit equipped with 15cm sIG 33 heavy infantry guns under SS-Hauptsturmführer Reiche. All these units at Friedenthal and Neustrelitz were immediately put on alert for deployment to the East.

The first contingent of Waffen-SS troops left Friedenthal at 0300-hrs on 31st January and arrived at Schwedt during that morning. Skorzeny himself arrived there about 0700-hrs. They found the town still in German hands, the six road bridges over the canal and river still intact, and the two waterways and the marshes in between frozen solid. However, the area was devoid of any German units capable of resisting an enemy attack. The replacement units that had been stationed at Schwedt – Pionier-Ersatz-Bataillon 12 and Panzergrenadier-Ersatz-Bataillone 3, 9 and 83 – had by this time all been sent eastwards to help save the situation after the collapse of Heeresgruppe A. This left the whole area virtually defenceless. The ground crew from the Luftwaffe airfield near Königsberg-Neumark had carried out a slipshod destruction of the airfield and then hastily moved westwards to avoid the onrush of the Red Army. The difficult military situation was made even worse by the flight of local civilian and Nazi Party authorities and by the hundreds of refugees moving in harsh winter conditions in search of safety west of the Oder.

What is commonly called the Oder bridge at Schwedt was actually the bridge over the Hohensaaten-Friedrichsthaler Wasserstrasse, the canal that runs parallel with the river. Construction of the canal began in 1906 but, delayed by the First World War, was not completed until 1926.

The main course of the Oder was spanned by the easternmost of the six bridges across the river's floodplain, the one at Nieder-Kränig. For the next four weeks, the span would form the bridgehead's only fixed connection with the safety of the west bank.

Part II. Defending the Oder • 69

The main town in the Schwedt bridgehead area was Königsberg-in-der-Neumark.

Realising that no Soviet forces had crossed the river in the Schwedt area, Skorzeny set up his command post in the village of Nieder-Kränig on the east bank and promptly began preparations for the inevitable clash. Reconnaissance patrols were sent across the river, sallying out deep into enemy-held territory to seek out and monitor the movement of the Soviet units, take and bring in prisoners for interrogation, and warn the main force of the incoming assault. An immediate evacuation of the civilian population was ordered, a task which Skorzeny delegated to the Stadtkommandant (town commandant) of Schwedt, a war-invalided but efficient Oberst, and to the town's Bürgermeister, Wilhelm Schrader-Rottmers. Stragglers from Wehrmacht units decimated in the east were gathered and sent to the military barracks in Schwedt where an assembly point had been set up to re-organise them into so-called Alarm-Einheite (emergency units). Over the following days several Alarm-Einheite battalions and companies would be formed, named after their respective commanders, and sent to reinforce the bridgehead.

In the meantime, an Organisation Todt labour unit, OT-Regiment 122 from Stettin – helped by civilian labourers recruited and organised by the NSDAP-Ortsgruppenleiters (Nazi Party local group leaders) from Schwedt and the surrounding villages – got to work on digging trenches, foxholes and machine-gun emplacements. With the help of the major commanding Pionier-Ersatz-Bataillon 12, Skorzeny staked out his bridgehead perimeter. They devised three lines of defence, each perimeter in a semi-circle progressively further from the eastern end of the Oder bridge.

Lying 17 kilometres east of the Oder, by the end of January 1945 the town was being flooded by refugees from all over the region desperately fleeing ahead of the advancing Soviet armies. (Alamy)

Königsberg is today Chojna in Poland and, although this is exactly the same view, not a single original building remains on the present-day market square. After the Soviets captured the town, they set fire to it as a retaliatory measure, three-quarters of Königsberg being destroyed as a result. Much of the ruined property was never rebuilt, every brick in this former German territory being carried off to be used in the reconstruction of Warsaw. In addition, the Polish people who moved in, resettled here from the former eastern part of Poland, for many years thought they were only going to be here temporarily as the Germans would no doubt soon reclaim it, or at some stage they might be able to return to their old homes (now in Lithuania, Belorussia and Ukraine). As a result, they never cared much about reconstructing buildings in their original style as has been the case in many towns in pre-war Poland. (Tomasz Zgoda)

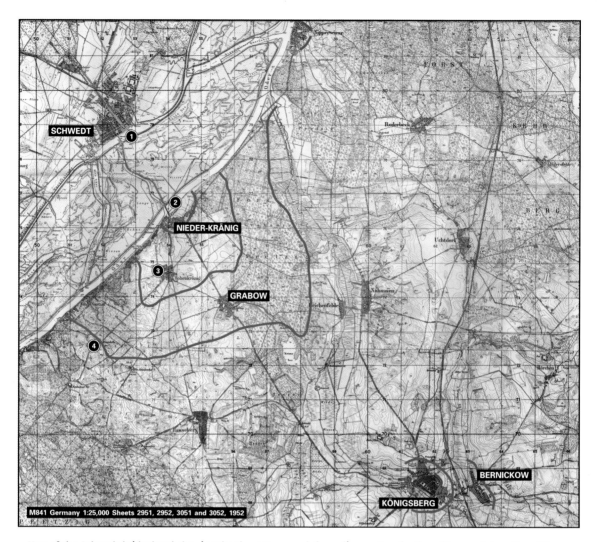

Map of the Schwedt bridgehead showing the three German defence lines set up by Kampfgruppe Schwedt and the outpost position at Königsberg. [1] Oder Canal Bridge. [2] Oder River Bridge. [3] Von Humbert Estate. [4] Raduhn Farm.
(Brigham Young University)

GERMAN DEFENCES

The outer ring started some four kilometres north of the Schwedt bridges at the confluence of the Oder with the small Rörike river, followed the wooded south bank of the Rörike south-east to Wachholderberge, passing north of the Krimo-See (a small lake) to cross the Grabow to Königsberg road, continuing on to Hills 42 and 40 where it turned south-west towards Hill 62.9, and from there across Hills 83.6 and 98.2 and via the Amalienhof Farm to the Elisenhöhe Farm where it crossed the Raduhn Farm to the Hohen-Kränig road, running through the flat fields to pass south of the village of Nieder-Saathen and then back to the Oder.

The middle line started at the Oder some two kilometres north of the Schwedt bridges, ran due east along the southern edge of the Peetzig/Röderbeck Forest, then veered south to cross the Nieder-Kränig to Grabow road west of the latter town, turning south-west to pass in front of the village of Hohen-Kränig (Krajnik Górny), cross the road between that village and the Raduhn Farm, and run on to Hill 99.4 where it turned due west to reach the Oder again near the so-called Thal der Liebe.

The third and innermost line ran in a semi-arc of about one kilometre around the eastern end of the Oder bridge, defending the crossing and the village of Nieder-Kränig. The lines were well sited and made the bridgehead difficult to attack, because the northern part was covered by dense forests and the line of the Rörike river, while the southern part had trenches located on hills overlooking open ground.

The River Oder and canal, frozen as they were, offered little in the way of an obstacle to an advancing enemy but the engineer major had his men blow gaps in the ice, reinstating the flow and thus creating a more resilient barrier to the Soviet advance.

As it turned out, Skorzeny's men had five days – from 31st January to 4th February – to prepare for the coming battle, to amass forces and to gather additional weapons. Initially, Kampfgruppe Schwedt, as it was now called, had only five main infantry components: in addition to SS-Fallschirmjäger Bataillon 600 and SS-Jagdverband Mitte with its supporting units, there were three Volkssturm (home guard) battalions. One was from Schwedt, raised locally and commanded by the town's Bürgermeister Schrader-Rottmers; the second was from Königsberg, led by its Bürgermeister Kurt Flöter; and the third strangely enough, came all the way from Hamburg, 400 kilometres away. Sent east to reinforce the Oder front it arrived in the sector on 4th February. Nearly 600 strong, it was a remarkably tough unit, comprising sturdy stevedores and dockworkers from the ocean port, well equipped and fully armed with rifles and Panzerfäuste.

In addition to infantry, Skorzeny needed heavy weapons. He had brought his six 15cm heavy infantry guns with him but clearly needed more. Told that no anti-tank guns were available, Skorzeny's supply officer, SS-Hauptsturmführer Reinhard Gerhard, scoured the region looking for means to bolster the force's firepower. He happened upon the Ardelt-Werke, an armaments factory in Eberswalde 50 kilometres to the south, which had been evacuated because of the approach of the Russians. From there he collected a dozen 7.5cm PaK 40 anti-tank guns plus a quantity of anti-tank rounds. From a dump near Frankfurt-an-der-Oder his men were able to purloin a large number of brand-new MG42 machine guns along with ammunition. A number of 2cm FlaK guns arrived from the Königsberg airfield. Two home-defence Flak battalions arrived with thirty-two 8.8cm and 10.5cm FlaK guns. Ten of these big FlaK guns were deployed inside the bridgehead, the others were set up on the western side of the river.

Kampfgruppe Schwedt had begun to take shape. As the battle developed, other units were temporarily assigned to it including several of the Alarm-Einheiten. By the time that the Soviets arrived the force available for the

An SS-Kriegsberichter (SS war reporter) by the name of Friedel Könnecke was present in the Schwedt bridgehead for most of February, exposing at least four rolls of film and taking a unique series of pictures of the battle. Here Skorzeny meets with two of his principal commanders in the bridgehead, SS-Obersturmbannführer Siegfried Milius (centre), the commander of SS-Fallschirmjäger-Bataillon 600, and SS-Obersturmführer Joachim Marcus (right), commander of the battalion's 3. Kompanie. The location is the Von Humbert Estate in Hohen-Kränig, the command post of SS-Jagdverband Mitte. In the first days of the bridgehead, the supply sergeant of SS-Jagdverband Mitte, SS-Oberscharführer Glas, discovered a depot full of winter camouflage clothing. Confiscating the entire stock, he had it distributed throughout Kampfgruppe Schwedt, making it, in Glas's words 'the unit best equipped with winter clothing on the entire Eastern Front'. Skorzeny is wearing the Winter-Wendetarn-Jacke, a jacket specially insulated for the winter, which could be reversed from splinter-pattern camouflage to plain white. (MNZS NI9-752)

defence numbered approximately 4,000-5,000 men. However, many of them were poorly armed and their fighting ability quite varied.

Skorzeny positioned his forces in the bridgehead as follows. Occupying the outer line was SS-Fallschirmjäger-Bataillon 600. Its 1. Kompanie commanded by SS-Obersturmführer Fritz Leifheit held the southern sector in front of Nieder-Saathen (Zaton Dolna), whilst 2. Kompanie under SS-Obersturmführer Walter Scheu defended the village of Grabow in the centre. To delay the enemy attack that was certain to come, an outpost position was set up in the town of Königsberg, some 13 kilometres further east and 17 kilometres from the Oder. This was held by 3. Kompanie under SS-Obersturmführer Joachim Marcus with some 50 troops under his command. The forward line was reinforced by the Volkssturm battalions from Königsberg and Hamburg. The northern part of the outer line, running along the Rörike river, was manned by the first of the new Alarm-Einheite,

The Von Humbert Estate before the war. The buildings visible in the wartime picture can be seen in the centre background.

Incredible as it may seem, nothing remains of the estate today. The heavily damaged buildings were all pulled down after the war and the bricks carried off to Warsaw.
(Tomasz Zgoda)

Bataillon Jacobs (with 863 men). Manning the inner lines were the SS hunter units, with SS-Jagdverband Mitte concentrating its forces around Nieder-Kränig and the composite company from SS-Jagdverband Nordwest defending the immediate area around the Oder bridges.

THE RED ARMY'S ARRIVAL

The Germans had organised their defence in the nick of time for already the enemy was advancing on the bridgehead. The Soviet 1st Mechanised Corps, part of the Second Guards Tank Army, was moving toward Königsberg from the southeast. Its mission was to capture the town, reach the Oder bridge at Nieder-Kränig and clear the east bank of German forces. The first encounters with reconnaissance patrols from Skorzeny's force occurred on 1st February at the small town of Bad Schönfliess (today Trzcińsko-Zdrój), eight kilometres east of Königsberg and 25 kilometres from Schwedt.

Part II. Defending the Oder • 75

Skorzeny (left) inspecting the positions on the east bank of the Oder with SS-Hauptsturmführer Dr Helmuth Slama from SS-Jagdverband Mitte.

They were standing on the river dike that runs between Nieder-Kränig and Nieder-Saathen. (Tomasz Zgoda)

It was in the early morning of the 4th, returning to his command post after a night at the front, that Skorzeny bumped into Königsberg's Bürgermeister, Kurt Flöter, who excitedly told him he had been waiting all night to report that all was lost in Königsberg. Judging that the man had deserted the troops under his command in the face of the enemy – which had caused the Königsberg Volkssturm to crumble and flee in panic – Skorzeny promptly had him arrested. Put before an SS court-martial chaired by Skorzeny himself, Flöter was publicly hanged from a tree on Schlossfreiheit, the park boulevard in front of the town castle, a sign hung around his neck declaring 'I, Kurt Flöter, am hanging here because I deserted my town'. The corpse was left dangling for five days and was seen by all of the troops passing through the town en-route for the bridgehead. The incident prompted a furious reaction from Martin Bormann, the Nazi Party secretary, who sent Gauleiter Emil Stürtz of Gau Mark-Brandenburg to tell Skorzeny that senior Party members could only be tried by a Party tribunal. Skorzeny retorted:

'We tried your man not as a Party official but as a soldier – are not cowardice and desertion punishable in Party leaders too?' In all, during the bridgehead fighting, Skorzeny had at least a dozen men – both soldiers and civilians – hanged for defeatism or desertion.

Late in the afternoon of 4th February, just as darkness was falling, T-34/85 tanks from the 49th Guards Tank Brigade (temporarily subordinated to the 1st Mechanised Corps) clashed with the SS paratroopers at Bernickow (Barnkowo), a village just two kilometres east of Königsberg. The first assault was repulsed but the Soviets soon resumed their attacks. In the meantime, the Hamburg Volkssturm battalion, defending Königsberg itself, faced another attack of Soviet tanks, this time by Shermans from the 219th Tank Brigade advancing south from Uchtdorf (Lisie Pole). Seven tanks from the brigade stormed into the town but five of them were destroyed by Panzerfäuste whereupon those remaining retreated. In all, the two Russian tank brigades lost ten tanks between them at this juncture.

Despite their initial successes, the defenders of Bernickow and Königsberg were soon outnumbered and outgunned. They fell back to the centre of town, behind the medieval walls, but they managed to hold out only until 0500-hrs on the 5th, at which point they pulled back to the bridgehead proper. There they took up positions in the outer trench line. Following the Soviet capture of the town, those German citizens who had remained were to suffer a terrible ordeal. They were robbed, murdered and driven out from their homes, and many women and girls were raped.

Skorzeny instituted a reign of terror in the bridgehead, court-martialling and hanging over a dozen men for desertion and cowardice, among them the Bürgermeister of Königsberg, Kurt Flöter, hanged from a tree in Schwedt on 4th February. Today, a plaque on Bahnhofstrasse still commemorates one of the victims, Panzergrenadier Norbert Robert: 'Here in March 1945 a young soldier was hanged by Fascists because he wanted peace.' (Schwedt.EU)

The Soviet tank forces pushed relentlessly on towards the Oder bridge but were stopped in Grabow by the SS paratroopers. Using buildings, fences and hedgerows for cover, the Fallschirmjäger stalked the Soviet tanks with Panzerfäuste and engaged the infantry with small-arms fire. One of those who fell during this battle was Lieutenant Oleg Matvejev, later awarded the Hero of the Soviet Union medal. Time and again the Soviets renewed their attacks until finally the Germans were pushed out of the village, falling back to the bridgehead's main trench line. A small force from the 219th Tank Brigade even managed to break through to within sight of the Oder bridge but, after losing one Sherman, had to pull back towards Reichenfelde (Garnowo). The Soviet advance came to standstill.

Skorzeny and Milius assigned part of Marcus's 3. Kompanie to assume the defence of Königsberg. Soon after they arrived in the town, a well-equipped Volkssturm (Home Guard) battalion arrived all the way from Hamburg to further reinforce the position. Here Marcus confers with what is probably the battalion commander, a police officer. This photo was taken before the battle started. (MNZS NI1-747)

COUNTER-ATTACK

The short lull in the fighting gave the Germans time to reinforce Kampfgruppe Schwedt with two batteries of assault guns from Sturmgeschütz-Brigade 210 (Major Dietrich Langel) and with Fallschirm-Panzer-Jagd-Bataillon 54, a paratroop anti-tank unit composed of 285 men. This reinforcement enabled them to regain much of the territory just lost. On 7th February, three German battalions – SS-Jagdverband Mitte, SS-Fallschirmjäger-Bataillon 600 and Fallschirm-Panzer-Jagd-Bataillon 54 – supported by the newly-arrived StuGs stormed Grabow. The village was defended by elements of the 35th Mechanised Brigade and 219th Tank Brigade. German superiority in guns and numbers left the Soviets with no chance to hold out against the assault. Immediately after they had recaptured the village, the German force split into two, one group moving south-east to capture the important crossroads of the Grabow–Königsberg and Reichenfelde–Hanseberg roads, while the other attacked toward Hanseberg (Krzymów) and forced elements of the 37th

Having arrived on 31st January, the Fallschirmjäger had five days to prepare for the Russian attack, which began in earnest on 5th February. As Könnecke's caption reads: 'The Soviets carry the battle into German land. Front and homeland bond together in an ever-growing common fate. Where yesterday the farmer or his wife worked in the fields now runs the main battle line, and German men defend the home soil with their own bodies. A farmer's wife brings a hot meal to SS-Fallschirmjäger that have taken up position in front of a village in Neumark.' These men belong to the battalion's 4. (schwere) Kompanie, the heavy weapons company, as is evidenced by the 8cm GrW 34 mortar in their pit. (MNZS NI8-645)

Mechanised Brigade to withdraw from the village. A quantity of very useful mortars, anti-tank guns, heavy machine guns and ammunition was captured.

The day held another surprise. Immediately after the recapture of Grabow, Skorzeny received a signal at his advanced command post that Reichsmarshall Hermann Göring, the commander-in-chief of the Luftwaffe, was in Schwedt, waiting to see him. Göring's grand estate Carinhall was only some 40 kilometres from the Oder and, from the first, Göring had shown a benevolent interest in the bridgehead, frequently telephoning Skorzeny to ask how it was going. It was at his behest that Fallschirm-Panzer-Jagd-Bataillon 54 had been sent to reinforce the position. Now the Reichsmarshall himself had come to visit the bridgehead. Clad in plain field-grey, without any medals, he went with Skorzeny almost up to the front line near Nieder-Kränig, doling out cigarettes and brandy, and showing a particular interest in the knocked-out Soviet tanks that stood around still burning. He made a point of visiting one of the 8.8cm Flak guns that were being used in an anti-tank role, congratulating the crew on their achievements. He also visited the command post of SS-Fallschirm-Bataillon 600 at Hohen-Kränig and it was well after dark before he departed.

Marcus set up an outpost position in the village of Bernickow, two kilometres east of Königsberg. It was here that Könnecke pictured two members of the 3. Kompanie 'following with their eyes the German fighters that are engaged in aerial combat with Soviet aircraft above them'. Many of the photos taken by Könnecke have the feel of being staged so it is difficult to say whether the action is real. (MNZS NI8-637)

This is one of the few instances where the comparison is confirmed by an existing building. The house in the background of Könnecke's photo is today hidden by a line of pine trees but it still remains unchanged in over 70 years. The cemetery seen behind the soldiers is still there. After the war Bernickow became Barnkowo and is today part of Chojna. (Tomasz Zgoda)

Two days after the recapture of Grabow, on 9th February, the SS paratroopers, supported by assault guns, moved even further and retook the forester's lodge near the Tanger-See. The Germans managed to bring in more of the Alarm-Einheite to man the outer line, the sector to the south of Grabow being occupied by Bataillon Zapf (767 strong), and the southern end of the bridgehead being taken over by Bataillon Aschenbach (486 strong). SS-Fallschirmjäger-Bataillon 600 now held the centre part of the line, from the Krimo-See to Hill 62.9, while SS-Jagdverband Mitte went into reserve around Nieder-Kränig.

The Soviets quickly recovered from the surprisingly strong German counter-stroke. They brought reinforcements forward and in turn staged their own counter-attack the following day. Heavy fighting raged along the Grabow–Königsberg road and on Hill 62.9. The Germans suffered heavy losses, particularly SS-Fallschirmjäger-Bataillon 600. Two company commanders – SS-Obersturmführer Joachim Marcus of 3. Kompanie, and SS-Obersturmführer Wilhelm Schmiedl of 2. Kompanie – were killed. 3. Kompanie, which took the brunt of the assault, had only 30 men standing by the end of the day.

Later the 37th Mechanised Brigade, with support of SU-122 assault guns from the 347th Guards Heavy Assault Gun Regiment, were sent to recapture Hanseberg. The Germans held on to it until the 11th when the village fell to the Red Army.

Overnight on 11th/12th February the 1st Mechanised Corps moved north and was replaced by units of the 8th Guards Mechanised Corps. This comprised the 20th and 21st Guards Mechanised Brigade, the latter supported by the 294th Penal Company. The Soviet units were fresh and they immediately resumed the attacks on the bridgehead but the German defenders put up a determined resistance and the line was not penetrated.

Fierce engagements on the flanks of the bridgehead continued into the 13th. At the northern end, a reconnaissance company from the 20th Guards Mechanised Brigade assaulted and captured the hamlet of Nipperwiese (Ognica). The weak Luftwaffe company defending the village proved no match for the Soviet infantry. Meanwhile, at the bridgehead's southern end a Soviet infantry company supported by ten T-34 tanks from the 21st Guards Mechanised Brigade was sent to capture the hamlet of Raduhn (Radun). The German outpost there was soon forced to pull back. Perhaps even worse, Kampfgruppe Schwedt's offensive capabilities were considerably weakened by the withdrawal of the two assault gun batteries from the bridgehead.

At 1600-hrs. – right in the middle of these desperate battles – Skorzeny received a signal from Heeresgruppe Weichsel, ordering him to report to Himmler right away. He decided to stay with his men until the Soviet attacks had been halted and only arrived at Himmler's command post at 2030-hrs. Himmler was furious and began berating him for being late and having disobeyed an order, but particularly for having refused to relieve a Luftwaffe officer who had given up Nipperwiese and withdrawn to the inner

Warily, they examine the area around the tank, clearly conscious of the potential dangers. (MNZS NI6-379)

When Bernickow and Königsberg were lost on 5th February, the Germans fell back on the village of Grabow, which was the keystone of the German main line of defence in the bridgehead. The Soviet tanks immediately followed up and in their first attack, despite fierce opposition from the Fallschirmjäger in close combat, they managed to drive the Germans out of the village. However, reinforced with newly-arrived assault guns, SS-Fallschirmjäger-Bataillon 600 managed to recapture it on the 7th and, although it was attacked many times after that, Grabow remained in German hands until the final evacuation of the bridgehead. Here SS-Obersturmführer Marcus (in the long leather motorcycle coat) and some of his men approach one of the T-34/85 tanks of the 49th Guards Tank Brigade that was knocked out or abandoned in Grabow during the fighting on 5th February. Note the soldier with telescopic sight on his rifle on the right. (MNZS NI8-678)

line. Skorzeny explained that he himself had ordered the officer to do so. Thereupon Himmler simmered down and invited Skorzeny, who had arrived dirty and in combat uniform, to dinner. Skorzeny sat through the meal and then quickly returned to the bridgehead, disgusted but having secured from Himmler a promise to send him another assault gun unit.

Grabow was the most-devastated village in the bridgehead, and it was only the parapet of the bridge over this nameless stream that allowed Tomasz to pinpoint the exact spot on what is today the DK26 in the centre of the village. The view is looking eastwards. (Tomasz Zgoda)

Part II. Defending the Oder • 83

SONNERNWENDE

The German counter-offensive in Pomerania finally got under way on 16th February, It had first been mooted by Himmler in his initial telephone order to Skorzeny on 31st January. Code-named Operation 'Sonnenwende', it was the last hope for the Germans to strike a significant blow at the Red Army and stop it before it could stage the final assault on Berlin.

The original idea for the offensive had been put forward by Generaloberst Heinz Guderian. The plan was to have a strong two-pronged attack by two armies. The 11. SS-Panzer-Armee in Pomerania would strike south from the Stettin area while the 6. SS-Panzer-Armee, freshly transferred from the Ardennes front, would launch a northward attack from the Gluben–Glogau area. Both armies were each to cover a distance of 70 kilometres

Könnecke's caption explains the German tactics: 'Small Stosstrupps (assault platoons) – paratroopers operating all by themselves – fight a bitter battle. Again and again, they attack the Soviets and keep them pinned down until the main force of their unit has deployed and stands ready for the planned counter-attack.' This picture was almost certainly taken in Grabow. (MNZS NI9-747)

84 • RED ARMY TOWARDS THE ODER – THEN AND NOW

Members of a motorised Stosstrupp on the outskirts of Grabow. Note the 'S' (which could stand either for Kampfgruppe Schwedt or Kampfgruppe 'Solar') on the mudguard of the Stoewer le.E.Pkw light passenger car. The soldier in the centre, armed with an MG42 machine gun, is wearing a Luftwaffe flying suit, which suggests he belonged to one of the companies formed from Luftwaffe ground personnel from the Königsberg airfield. Just visible behind him is Obersturmführer Marcus, recognisable by his long leather coat and dented officer's cap. The paratrooper on the right is carrying an MKb 42 assault rifle. (MNZS NI9-742)

in order to affect a link-up, cutting off the forward formations of the First Byelorussian Front. However, in early February Hitler dismissed the plan for a double envelopment, deciding instead to use the 6. SS-Panzer-Armee in an operation to relieve Budapest.

He now opted for a 'small solution', a single-prong attack, whereby the 11. SS-Panzer-Armee would strike south from Pomerania with two corps from the region of Stargard and link up with the Oder bridgeheads. On the left, the III. SS-Panzerkorps would drive south via Arnswalde all the way to Küstrin and on the right the XXXIX. Panzerkorps would drive from south of Stargard via Pyritz towards Schwedt. They could then link up with troops driving up from Skorzeny's bridgehead. This would entail a single drive of 70 kilometres, half the distance that would have been achieved in the original plan. If it succeeded, it would relieve several besieged cities, result in the destruction of all Soviet troops west of the drive, and considerably shorten the German front line.

However, after the first few days it was already clear that the offensive had failed. The attacking forces only managed to get to the surrounded towns of Arnswalde, Pyritz and Bahn – a penetration of a mere ten kilometres at its deepest. The force was too weak to penetrate toward Küstrin. A potential opportunity to turn the tide of war on the Eastern Front had been lost. On 19th February, Himmler stopped the offensive, a decision confirmed by a formal Hitler directive on the 21st. With the collapse of 'Sonnenwende', the main reason for holding on to the Schwedt bridgehead appeared to be redundant. However, Heeresgruppe Weichsel must have considered the continued German presence on the Oder's east bank to have some value as it did not give orders for its evacuation.

'From their muddy holes in the ground, the paratroopers observe the open expanse across which the Soviets are expected to attack.' (MNZS NI8-633)

86 • RED ARMY TOWARDS THE ODER – THEN AND NOW

Battalion commander Milius (in white fur jacket) congratulates men of the 3. Kompanie with the successful defence of Grabow. 'Of 30 enemy tanks deployed for a breakthrough, these six NCOs of an assault platoon destroyed 16 with Panzerfäuste.' On the right stands Obersturmführer Marcus, the company commander, now wearing a green M40 parachute smock. Barely visible behind Milius and shaking the hand of one of the men is SS-Hauptscharführer Walter Hummel, the leader of the battalion scout platoon. Marcus died on 9th February, which narrows when this picture may have been taken. (MNZS NI8-489)

On 17th February, Division Schwedt, as it had been renamed, launched an assault on the Amalienhof Farm (Krzymówek). Thanks to support provided by the battery from Sturmgeschütz-Brigade 210, two Soviet tanks, two anti-tank guns and six mortars were knocked out. There was also activity on the northern flank where the newly-arrived III. Bataillon of Fallschirmjäger-Regiment 26 (Major Hans-Heinrich Hacker) re-occupied Nipperwiese, which had been abandoned by the Soviets.

WITHDRAWAL

At this time another switch of forces occurred on the Soviet side, the 8th Guards Mechanised Corps was withdrawn and its positions taken over by 129th Rifle Corps. This comprised the 132nd Rifle Division (498th, 605th and 712th Rifle Regiments) and the 143rd Rifle Division (487th, 635th and 800th Rifle Regiments). Over the next few days both sides went over to the

While Grabow was attacked by the 49th Guards Tank Brigade, other units of the 1st Guards Mechanised Corps streamed past to the south, aiming for the Oder bridge. A column of Sherman tanks (supplied to the Russians under Lend-Lease) from the 37th Mechanised Brigade was intercepted on the Raduhn to Hohen-Kränig road, close to the turnoff to Raduhn Farm, and here two of the Shermans were destroyed. A German Propaganda-Kompanien cameraman recorded the scene after the battle, as evidenced by these stills from the Deutsche Wochenschau newsreel of 16th March, 1945, which included a montage on the 'heroic defence' of the Schwedt bridgehead.
(Deutsche Wochenschau)

The electricity post has gone but the same cobbled road still leads through the woods to Raduhn. (Tomasz Zgoda)

defence, limiting themselves to reconnaissance patrols. With all quiet on the front, snipers came to the fore, the marksmen of the SS-Scharfschützen-Zug claiming 260 'kills' by 24th February. Operating chiefly from no man's land, they also established cleverly camouflaged positions on the large ice-floes that were floating down the Oder river, a thaw having set in on 12th February.

After seven days holding Nipperwiese, III. Bataillon of Fallschirmjäger-Regiment 26 was relieved by a company from Bataillon Aschenbach. The paratroopers were withdrawn and later sent to Breslau to help defend the encircled and besieged city.

Two days later, on the 26th, the Soviets launched their final offensive to liquidate the bridgehead. In the south, the 605th Rifle Regiment, supported by ISU-122 assault guns from the 334th Guards Heavy Assault Gun Regiment, attacked towards Hills 66.4, 99.4, Hohen-Kränig and Hill 81.5. The fights raged all day but by nightfall they had only managed to wrestle Hill 81.5 from the Germans. In the centre, following a preliminary artillery barrage, two battalions from the 487th Rifle Regiment and one from the 800th Rifle Regiment launched an attack on Grabow supported by four IS-2 tanks from the 70th Guards Heavy Tank Regiment. The Soviets met stiff opposition and did not break through the German lines. The only important gain was in the north where two companies of the 635th Rifle Regiment, supported by four SU-76 assault guns from the 1416th Assault Gun Regiment, recaptured Nipperwiese. The assault was a disappointment, the attacks by both divisions making only limited progress.

That day, Skorzeny handed over command of his Kampfgruppe to SS-Obersturmbannführer Hans Kempin, previously in command of the 547. Volksgrenadier-Division. Having been working practically non-stop since deploying to the bridgehead, Skorzeny had been relieved of his duties on the

The same newsreel item showed men of Kampfgruppe Schwedt on parade for an award ceremony, Skorzeny's speech being sound-recorded: 'The Russian has learned to fear us. Ivan can be beaten too, as our gang has proven. I am pleased to be able to award some of you with the Panzer-Vernichtungs-Abzeichen (tank destruction award).' Skorzeny then calls out the name of a Stabsfeldwebel Kunze and hands him the badge. Next, Kunze describes his act: 'A messenger comes to me. Stabsfeldwebel, the Russians are here. I said, OK, be calm, boy, it will not be so bad. I grabbed my Panzerfaust and already saw the colossus, about ten, twelve metres in front of me. It was a T-34. I let it come a little closer, put my Panzerfaust on the shoulder and calmly pressed the trigger. And, bang, there it lay. The crew jumped out immediately and I at once fired with my machine pistol after them and cut them down as well.' (Deutsche Wochenschau)

The ceremony took place in Schwedt, more particular on Lindenallee, the tree-lined park avenue on the west bank of the Oder behind the Schloss. The castle, ruined in the 1945 battle, was blown up by the East German authorities in 1962, being replaced in 1974-78 by a modern theatre hall, but the old castle garden remains, re-landscaped and named the Europäischer Hugenottenpark. (Tomasz Zgoda)

SS-Kriegsberichter Könnecke must have stayed in the Grabow sector until the end for, although the bridgehead was abandoned on 1st March, the captions of his later pictures were dated March 1945. This one reads: 'SS Fallschirmjäger are attacking. The SS paratroopers have firmly established themselves in trenches that have just been cleared of Bolsheviks in close combat and now prepare to stave off any enemy counter-attack.' Note that snow has fallen.
(MNZS NI8-646)

The line of electricity posts in the background enabled Tomasz Zgoda to identify the location as being in the fields west of Grabow, close to the Grabow to Nieder-Kränig road.
(Tomasz Zgoda)

21st but had stayed on another five days before allowing himself a break.

The following day, 27th February, Division Schwedt received orders to prepare evacuation of the bridgehead. According to the plan, the first to leave would be the artillery and heavy flak then, overnight on the 1st/2nd March the infantry, armour and covering units were to follow. Before the last German troops left, all the disabled tanks were mined, and buildings booby-trapped. The retreat went well and was unnoticed by the Soviets. The last unit leaving the Oder's east bank was SS-Fallschirmjäger-Bataillon 600. Due to a lack of explosives, the bridge at Nieder-Kränig was only partially destroyed.

Part II. Defending the Oder • 91

'Where ten minutes ago the Soviets were sitting, the signal platoon of the SS-Fallschirmjäger has now set up.' (MNZS NI8-627)

On the night of 1st/2nd March, with the Soviets having launched their final offensive, Division Schwedt evacuated the Oder bridgehead, successfully withdrawing all its troops to the west bank and blowing the bridge at Nieder-Kränig behind it. Due to the lack of explosives, only two spans were destroyed. (O. Hartmut Collection)

Today a new bridge crosses the river at the same point, which is also now the frontier between Germany and Poland. (Tomasz Zgoda)

For their actions in the bridgehead, three SS officers were awarded the Deutsche Kreuz in Gold: SS-Hauptsturmführer Werner Hunke (the Kampfgruppe's operations officer), SS-Hauptsturmführer Siegfried Milius and, posthumously, SS-Obersturmführer Joachim Marcus.

The battles that had raged for the Schwedt bridgehead for nearly a month had been very costly for both sides. Soviet casualties amounted to around 700 men killed and between 1,400 and 2,000 wounded. Soviet losses in armour are hard to determine but are assumed to be between 30 and 40 tanks and assault guns. German casualty figures were also high, some 800 men having been killed and wounded. Practically every town and village in the bridgehead was reduced to rubble, Königsberg losing 75 per cent of its buildings and Grabow 60 per cent.

The month-long battle left most of the towns and villages in the bridgehead in ruins. Although Königsberg had suffered only minor damage during the actual fighting for the town, between 4th and 5th February. This was not to remain the case. Around 75 per cent of the town was ravaged by fire after Soviet soldiers set light to many of the buildings on 16th February. This is how the centre of the town looked after the rubble had been removed, with the burned-out shell of the 15th-century Town Hall in the centre. (Tadeusz Bialecki)

In post-war years Königsberg – now Polish and renamed Chojna – was rebuilt in a much more-sober architectural style. The Town Hall was reconstructed in 1986, one of only two buildings in town restored to their original state.
(Tomasz Zgoda)

The other was the 14th-century Sankt-Marien-Kirche, restored in German-Polish co-operation between 1994 and 2003. (Wartime picture from Tadeusz Bialecki – comparison from Tomasz Zgoda)

THE ZEHDEN BRIDGEHEAD

BUILDUP

Contemporaneously with the creation of the defence of the Schwedt bridgehead, Heeresgruppe Weichsel decided to create two other bridgeheads across the Oder. The first was twenty-five kilometres further to the south, near the town of Zehden (today Cedynia in Poland), and the other was at the village of Zäckerick (Siekierki), seven kilometres to the south-east. Both

The Zehden bridgehead over the Oder, 25 kilometres south of that at Schwedt, was originally linked to the latter by a narrow strip of land on the east bank, thinly held by a small security force. However, from 14th February onwards this strip was cut, separating the two bridgeheads. The line shows the furthest position reached by the Germans on 9th March. (Brigham Young University)

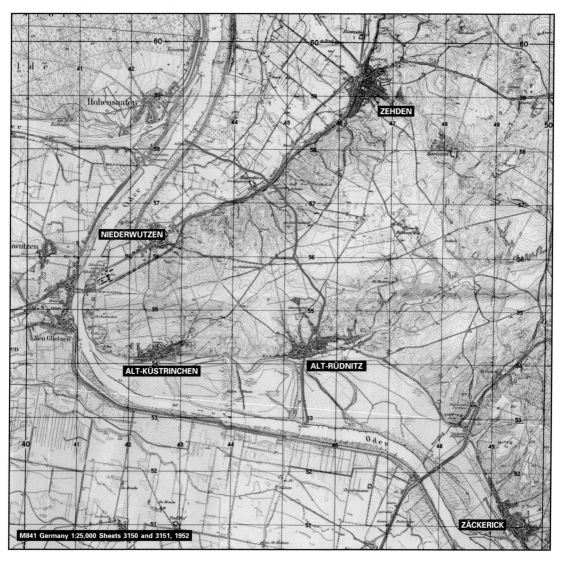

The bridgehead's only link with the west bank was the road bridge at Niederwutzen. Completed in 1904 it was known as the Von Saldern-Brücke after its constructor, Werner Kurt Aschwin von Saldern. In addition to motor traffic it carried the Bad Freienwalde to Zehden train line. When on 6th March, a lucky hit by a Soviet artillery round hit the bridge's explosive charge and blew up the western part of the span, the bridgehead lost its only fixed connection with the west bank. From then on, all supplies and reinforcements had to be ferried across. Later a narrow footbridge was constructed.

towns are on the east side of the river. The Zehden bridgehead was served by a single road bridge located at the village of Niederwutzen (today the Polish border town of Osinów Dolny) and the Zäckerick one was connected to the west bank by a road and rail bridge. Both were small footholds, the one at Zehden being some six kilometres by four kilometres and the one at Zäckerick even smaller.

Again the Germans acted faster than the Soviet armoured units and within a short time managed to set up defences that survived the first Russian attacks. Little is known about the German units that first held the Zehden bridgehead. Apparently they consisted of the vestiges of some disparate Wehrmacht units and some Volkssturm troops cobbled together, possessing only small arms and Panzerfäuste with which to defend themselves.

The first Soviet forces arrived in the area on 31st January and into 1st February. However, it was only a weak tank spearhead that had outrun its infantry support. They were low on fuel, short of ammunition, exhausted and incapable of taking Zehden or the Niederwutzen bridge without backup. It therefore served simply to carry out a reconnaissance of the area. The leading elements of 82nd Rifle Division (210th, 250th and 601st Rifle Regiments) began to arrive on the 2nd. They were able to occupy Grüneberg (Golice), just south-east of Zehden, and Zäckerick and Alt-Blessin (Stary Bleszyn), which were further south, close to the Oder and undefended. With

Rebuilt in 1952-57, the bridge – which after the war connected East Germany with Poland – was initially exclusively for military use by Warsaw Pact forces, being closed to all other traffic. It was only opened for general use in 1993. (Tomasz Zgoda)

Part II. Defending the Oder • 97

just 3,000 battle-weary troops, the division was in no position to launch an immediate attack, for the moment it limited itself to setting up a defence perimeter around its gains.

The first reinforcements to arrive were on the German side. Marine-Schützen-Brigade Nord arrived on 4th February. It was a unit made up of Kriegsmarine soldiers from the Wilhelmshaven area under the command of Konteradmiral Hans Hartmann. They had been sent via Angermünde to help establish a line on the Oder and the force was composed of three regiments of four battalions each. Shortly it would be renamed 1. Marine-Division. They lacked any infantry combat experience, had little transport, no engineers, no reconnaissance unit and what few artillery pieces they had were a melange of different types, some of which were of Soviet origin. Their presence at least added numbers to the defence. Initially these naval troops remained west of the Oder, taking up positions along the river bank.

Also on the 4th a revised command structure was implemented. The 'Oder-Korps', under Generalleutnant Günther Krappe, assumed command of the units defending the northern Oder sector. From north to south these were Kampfgruppe Klossek; SS-Kampfgruppe Skorzeny; and Hartmann's Marine-Schützen-Brigade Nord. The corps was directly subordinated to Heeresgruppe Weichsel. On 17th February command of the corps would be taken over by SS-Obergruppenführer Erich von dem Bach-Zelewski.

On the morning of 5th February, a strong reconnaissance from the 5th Guards Motorcycle Regiment and the 37th Mechanised Brigade, comprising three Sherman tanks, five armoured carriers and a rifle company, was sent forward to capture Zehden. The Germans resisted on the outskirts of the town but were soon forced back. However, a further Soviet advance was halted on the bridgehead's main line of defence, which ran in a shallow semi-arc from a point just north of where the Alte Oder flows into with the Oder itself, then southwards to the village of Alt-Rüdnitz. The key position in this line was Hill 60.6 which the Germans held, giving them a position from which they were able to observe the Soviet lines.

Following an inspection visit by Göring on the 7th, the newly renamed 1. Marine-Division sent Marine-Infanterie-Regiment 4 over into the bridgehead with orders to take up positions protecting the Niederwutzen bridge. The regiment was commanded by Kapitän zur See Gert Hasse and comprised Marine-Bataillone 310, 314 and 316. Shortly after, elements of four further battalions (Marine-Bataillone 302, 303, 304 and 305) also crossed the river to establish a security line linking up with the Schwedt bridgehead further north. The line now ran from Raduhn in the north via Peetzig and Bellichen to Zehden.

Further reinforcements were also arriving. Anti-aircraft batteries from FlaK-Regiment 145 of the 27. Flak-Division under Major Erich Krebs were sent into the bridgehead to set up an anti-tank screen. They were equipped with Soviet 85mm anti-aircraft guns converted to 88mm calibre in order to use German ammunition.

The first regular troops manning the Zehden bridgehead belonged to the Marine-Schützen-Brigade, soon renamed 1. Marine-Division. Attached to the unit was an official Kriegsmarine photographer-cameraman, Marine-Kriegsberichter Gerhard Garms, who chiefly took black-and-white photos but also shot rare colour film. This is the road junction just east of the Oder bridge. The two StuG III assault guns belong to Sturmgeschütz-Brigade 210, two batteries of which supported the bridgehead garrison from 13th February to 5th March. (Gerhard Garms)

This still from Garms's footage gives a better view of the Niederwutzen cellulose factory, which appears in the background. Kriegsmarine soldiers are crossing the Bad Freienwalde to Zehden railway line. As the road sign indicates, Berlin is only 63 kilometres away along Reichsstrasse 158. (Gerhard Garms)

Today, this area is covered by a huge shopping complex, much frequented by Germans from just across the border. Surprisingly, the factory survived all the ravages of war and nowadays houses many stalls. (Tomasz Zgoda)

The respite for the Germans continued, and on the 13th, two batteries from Major Langel's Sturmgeschütz-Brigade 210, equipped with StuG III and StuH 42 assault guns, further increased the German strength.

On the Soviet side, the 5th Guards Motorcycle Regiment and the 37th Mechanised Brigade in the Zehden sector were relieved by troops from the 19th Guards Mechanised Brigade, part of the 8th Guards Mechanised Corps. During this period, both sides limited themselves to reconnaissance and sporadic artillery fire.

The thinly-manned security line connecting the Schwedt and Zehden bridgeheads was subject to some heavy fighting between 11th and 14th February. The four German naval battalions holding Raduhn, Peetzig and Bellichen suffered worrying losses, which led to a decision to evacuate that part of the bridgehead and pull the units back across the Oder.

THE GATHERING STORM

The uneasy stalemate could not last. On 15th February, troops of the 210th Rifle Regiment opened an attack on the Zäckerick bridgehead in an attempt to capture the nearby bridge. The German force holding the town were too weak to withstand the assault but the Kriegsmarine soldiers came swiftly to their aid. Supported by assault guns, they managed to establish contact with Zäckerick's defenders and hold open a corridor through which they could retreat towards the Zehden bridgehead. As this was happening, infantry of the 601st Rifle Regiment broke into Alt-Rüdnitz but, without armour support, were no match for the Germans and were quickly ejected from the village. Overnight the Zäckerick bridgehead was successfully evacuated. The Zehden bridgehead had now shrunk to an area some four kilometres square.

Fighting died down again until 22nd February when the 2nd Battalion of the 601st Rifle Regiment launched a fresh assault on the bridgehead. Assisted by strong artillery fire and fighter-bomber strikes, the attack was assisted by six tanks from the 19th Guards Mechanised Brigade. After some initial success the attack faltered and was stopped.

Reconnaissance patrols, harassing artillery fire and sniping characterised the following few days. During this lull in the fighting the Soviets adopted psychological tactics in order to undermine the defenders' morale. Broadcasting from loudspeakers, the Soviets called on Germans to surrender: 'German soldiers, stop the fight! Your prisoners are with us. The password for those coming over to us is "Moscow"!'

The problems of using naval personnel as infantry persisted. The commander of 1. Marine-Division, Konteradmiral Hartmann, was of the opinion that the formation should remain manned entirely by Kreigsmarine personnel, despite the inadequacies of the formation's organisations. A Wehrmacht chief of staff, Generalmajor Wilhelm Bleckwenn was foisted on him at which point Hartmann resigned. Bleckwenn took over command on 28th February. The division was then switched out of the line to be replaced

One of the chimneys is hit by Soviet artillery.
(Gerhard Garms)

The chimney was pulled down after the war and never rebuilt.
(Tomasz Zgoda)

with Division z.b.V. 610. The first four battalions had moved out overnight on 2nd/3rd of March. The naval division was transferred 50 kilometres northwards, to the Oder positions at Greifenhagen. Only Marine-Bataillone 310 and 316 of Marine-Infanterie-Regiment 4 remained behind at Zehden, no longer in the bridgehead but taking up positions along the Oder's west bank. They would move northward and re-join their parent division on 10th March.

The Division z.b.V. 610 was raised on 26th January under the commanded of Generalleutnant Hubert Lendle. It was originally formed of battalions from several SS police regiments. The remnants of Kampfgruppe Skorzeny, by then withdrawn from Schwedt, were also added to its establishment. After being pulled out of the Schwedt bridgehead on 2nd March, they had marched to Heinersdorf, halfway between Frankfurt-an-der-Oder and Berlin. Here they were re-organised into what was named SS-Regiment 'Solar' and put under the command of SS-Hauptsturmführer Milius. The regiment

Part II. Defending the Oder • 101

Nearby, Garms filmed Kriegsmarine gunners firing a captured Russian Model 1927 76,2mm field howitzer, known to the Germans as 7,62cm Infanterie-Kanone-Haubitze 290 (r). It probably belonged to the 4. Kompanie of Marine-Bataillon 306. (Gerhard Garms)

The old railway line has been lifted and the spot where the gun stood is now part of the shopping centre's car park. (Tomasz Zgoda)

102 • RED ARMY TOWARDS THE ODER – THEN AND NOW

consisted of I. Bataillon (SS-Fallschirmjäger-Bataillon 600), still able to muster 500 men and now commanded by SS-Obersturmführer Leifheit; II. Bataillon (SS-Jagdverband Mitte) commanded by SS-Hauptsturmführer Fucker; the heavy infantry gun company of SS-Obersturmführer Reiche; the armoured reconnaissance company under SS-Obersturmführer Schwerdt, the sniper platoon under SS-Untersturmführer Wilscher, plus a signal and a supply company. On 5th March SS-Regiment 'Solar' crossed into the bridgehead, relieving the last remaining troops of the 1. Marine-Division. SS-Jagdverband Mitte occupied the sector north of the line Hühnerpfühle–Grüneberg, and the SS paratroopers took over the sector south of there. Milius deployed two of his 15cm heavy guns in the bridgehead, leaving the other four on the west bank. By this time the assault guns of Sturmgeschütz-Brigade 210 were no longer present, having been withdrawn on the evening of the 5th. Only the 8.8cm guns of Flak-Regiment 145 remained, with some positioned inside the bridgehead and others on the river's west bank. Late the following day four StuGs from Heeres-Sturmartillerie-Brigade 184 (Hauptmann Günter Liethmann) arrived. They would remain in the bridgehead until the end. The force defending the area around Zehden had shrunk to around 1,200 men.

Soviet operations resumed on 6th March, with the intention of clearing the bridgehead. 82nd Rifle Division launched an all-out attack on the bridgehead and were able to capture the crucial Hill 60.6. However, their success was short-lived. On 9th March, the SS units counter-attacked and, with the support of the artillery and assault guns, managed to push the front line back one kilometre eastwards, inflicting heavy casualties on the Soviets, re-taking Hill 60.6 and Alt-Rüdnitz and restoring their defensive positions.

However, the survival of the bridgehead was decisively weakened by a freak incident. Due to an omission by the demolition officer of Bau-Pionier-Bataillon 257, the Oder bridge at Niederwutzen was still wired with explosives. On the evening of 6th March, a chance shot from the Soviet artillery scored a direct hit, setting off the explosives and the bridge was partially blown up.

The reasons for holding on to the bridgehead had already become very questionable after the failure of the 'Sonnenwende' operation. By this point it had become practically suicidal. The only connections with the west bank were a small ferry and later a makeshift footbridge. From the beginning it had been clear that the bridgehead was too small to serve as springboard for a counter-offensive and that the Soviet forces surrounding it were too strong to push back. Plainly, the Soviets could not tolerate the presence of German troops on the Oder's east bank before it could implement the final advance on Berlin. Thus the fate of the bridgehead was sealed.

For most of March the front line did not move at all. Once again, the snipers came to the fore, Wilscher's marksmen claiming 248 hits. The most effective among them are recorded as SS-Rottenführer Elmo Scheffel and SS-Sturmmann Pieter Beuckels, with 60 'kills' each.

Two kilometres south of Niederwutzen, Garms filmed this view of the village of Alt-Küstrinchen and the wide water expanse of the overflowing Oder river. (Gerhard Garms)

As in the Schwedt bridgehead, most villages in the Zehden bridgehead suffered severely in the fighting. Thick vegetation today masks the view at this point so this comparison was taken in the middle of the village. (Tomasz Zgoda)

The 250th Rifle Regiment conducted a reconnaissance in force towards Hill 60.6 on 25th March. They were supported by SU-76 self-propelled guns of the 1416th Assault Gun Regiment and by artillery from the 146th and 795th Artillery Regiments. German reports claimed that the Soviets were also supported by some 15-20 tanks and assault guns. After a ten-minute artillery barrage, the 1st Battalion moved against the southern slope of Hill 60.6, capturing the first trench line. The 2nd Battalion was not so successful, massed machine-gun and mortar fire halting it before the first line of barbed-wire. In all, the Germans managed to destroy four tanks and assault guns. After dark the Soviet infantry withdrew but it was now clear to the Germans that the defence of the bridgehead was in its final few days.

The village of Alt-Rudnitz formed the south-eastern anchor of the bridgehead. It was from here that the Kriegsmarine soldiers and assault guns launched an attack on 15th February towards the village of Zäckerick, four kilometres to the south-east, to bring back the endangered defenders of the small German foothold there. The wall of bricks served to shield movement on the road from observation.
(Gerhard Garms)

Alt-Rudnitz is today called Stara Rudnica and these houses now stand at its western end.
(Google)

Part II. Defending the Oder • 105

ONE LAST PUSH

At 1415-hrs the following afternoon, the final Soviet attack was launched. Russian guns and Polish mortars laid down preparatory fire and Soviet Il-2 Sturmovik ground-attack aircraft struck at the German main defensive line and their artillery positions, further cratering the landscape. Both Soviet divisions began advancing on a broad front at 1500-hrs.

The 143rd Rifle Division attacked the northern half, from the Oder to a hill located 400 metres west of the main crossroads in front of the bridgehead. Armoured support was provided by 70th Guards Heavy Tank Regiment, 1825th Assault Gun Regiment and 1804th Heavy Assault Gun Regiment. They also had artillery cover from the 305th Guards Mortar Regiment and 425th Artillery Regiment, the latter detached from the 132nd Rifle Division. The advance captured the first trench line, inflicting heavy losses on SS-Jagdverband Mitte but the attack ran out of steam by 1700-hrs, halting whilst still half a kilometre east of the Hill 60.6 feature.

Young Flak gunners firing a captured 85mm Russian anti-aircraft gun. Converted to 88mm calibre, the gun was known in the Wehrmacht as a FlaK 8.5/8.8cm 39 (r). Gun and crew probably belonged to Flak-Regiment 145 of the 27. Flak-Division, which arrived in the bridgehead on 7th February. (Gerhard Garms)

StuH 42 assault howitzers and a StuG III assault gun from Sturmgeschütz-Brigade 210 near Alt-Küstrinchen. This unit was the mainstay of the German defence in the bridgehead from 13th February to 5th March.
(Gerhard Garms)

Part II. Defending the Oder • 107

The same SP guns in position behind two Panzerfaust-armed soldiers. StuG-Brigade 210 was relieved by four StuG IIIs from Sturm-Artillerie-Brigade 184, which however ended up cut off when the Niederwutzen bridge went up behind them on 6th March.
(Gerhard Garms)

Much of the Zehden bridgehead comprised bare sandy hills, which gave the defenders the upper hand.
(Tomasz Zgoda)

Men of the 1. Marine-Division moving into the line and (right) firing a Model 1934 8cm mortar in the Zehden bridgehead.
(Gerhard Garms)

108 • RED ARMY TOWARDS THE ODER – THEN AND NOW

The 82nd Rifle Division moved forward in the sector between the unnamed hill and the western outskirts of Alt-Rüdnitz. Their support was provided by the 1416th Assault Gun Regiment and 20th Flame-thrower Battalion. Covering fire was provided by 460th Mortar Regiment and 305th Guards Mortar Regiment. They ran into flanking fire from machine-guns located on Hill 60.6 which exacted heavy casualties on the Soviet troops. Consecutive attacks by both divisions accomplished nothing and with nightfall the fighting died down.

The following day, 27th March, the two Soviet divisions launched what

Part II. Defending the Oder • 109

On 5th March the 1. Marine-Division was relieved by SS-Regiment 'Solar', comprising the same SS units that until three days earlier had fought under Skorzeny in the Schwedt bridgehead: SS-Fallschirmjäger-Bataillon 600 and SS-Jagdverband Mitte. Very few pictures exist of the SS troops in the Zehden bridgehead. Here, SS-Hauptsturmführer Karl Fucker (right), the commander of SS-Jagdverband Mitte, interrogates a Russian prisoner (with fur cap).

SS-Untersturmführer Jochen Wichmann, the commander of the Jagdverband's 2. Kompanie, pictured in the bridgehead. Behind him is a US Jeep, captured from the Americans and used by Skorzeny's troops since the Ardennes offensive. Regiment 'Solar' held the Zehden bridgehead for another three weeks, being finally driven out by a massive Russian attack on the 27th, suffering heavy casualties in their last-minute retreat across the river.

turned out to be the decisive assault. At 1130-hrs a barrage fell on the German positions using all available guns and mortars within range. Half an hour later infantry, tanks and assault guns, stormed toward the enemy. German resistance had clearly begun to falter and was less obstinate than it had been the previous day. Both divisions managed to take the first and the second trench lines, pushing the defenders back toward the Oder. By 1400-hrs a co-ordinated action by both formations succeeded in taking Hill 60.6.

With the fall of the crucial hill, all organised German defence crumbled. After dark, Hauptsturmführer Milius – without prior approval from his superiors – ordered all troops to evacuate the bridgehead. The four StuGs of Heeres-Sturmartillerie-Brigade 184, their retreat cut off by the blown bridge, defended the ferry site at Niederwutzen till the end, knocking out 12 tanks and two self-propelled guns. Most of SS-Jagdverband Mitte managed to withdraw with the help of the makeshift footbridge. SS-Fallschirmjäger-Bataillon 600 was not so lucky and its soldiers had to swim across the icy river. Many were taken prisoner. By 2200-hrs all resistance in the bridgehead had ended. Milius feared a court-martial for his unsanctioned withdrawal but instead he received a glowing commendation from Generaloberst Gotthard Heinrici, who had taken over command of Heeresgruppe Weichsel on 21st March. Instead of the court-martial he found himself promoted to SS-Sturmbannführer.

Casualties after the two months of fighting for the Zehden bridgehead mirrored those at Schwedt. The Kriegsmarine units reported 48 men killed, 270 wounded and 44 missing – a total of 362. Out of the 1,200 soldiers defending the bridgehead in March, 790 were left on the Oder's east bank or drowned while retreating. In addition, four assault guns and at least five flak guns were lost. The Soviets incurred even higher losses with approximately 700 killed and probably two to three times as many wounded and missing. They had lost around 30 guns and 24 armoured fighting vehicles.

The desolate hills of the former battleground today. (Tomasz Zgoda)

Part II. Defending the Oder • **111**

PART III.
FESTUNG KÜSTRIN

LAST DAYS BEFORE THE SIEGE

Generalmajor Adolf Raegener, a seasoned soldier who had lost a leg before Moscow in 1941, was appointed Festungskommandant (Fortress Commander) for Küstrin. His task was far from simple and was not made easier by the

The city of Küstrin (today Kostrzyn nad Odra in Poland) lies at the confluence of the Oder and Warthe rivers, some 65 kilometres east of Berlin. For centuries it was the most-important stronghold guarding the Oder crossing towards Germany's capital.

The original settlement, the Altstadt (Old Town), located on the peninsula between the

Under siege by two Soviet armies, Küstrin's garrison doggedly held out for over two months, persevering even after the Russians finally completed their encirclement of the city on 22nd March. It took two major offensives, one in early March to capture the part of the city on the east bank of the Warthe, and another in late March to capture the rest, before the German defenders were finally subdued. This aerial shot of the ruined city was taken after the end of the battle. On the left is the Altstadt (old town), with the Ravelin August-Wilhelm and the Kietz Gate in the foreground, and in the background, across the Warthe river, is the Neustadt (new town). (Muzeum Twierdzy Kostrzyn)

fact that, during the last days of January, Küstrin was flooded with refugees from the eastern provinces, mostly the Warthegau and Mark Brandenburg. Hermann Körner, the Bürgermeister (Mayor) of Küstrin, who was also the NSDAP-Kreisleiter (Nazi Party District Leader), was responsible for civilian and party affairs and for organising the local Volkssturm (home guard).

Küstrin's garrison at that time consisted of a miscellany of soldiers from reserve units, training and replacement units, plus stragglers that had managed to reach the city before the Soviets' arrival. By 22nd February, it numbered 8,196 men and included a Festungs-Stab (fortress command staff), Festungs-Infanterie-Bataillon 1450, Panzergrenadier-Ersatz-Bataillon 50, three Marsch-Bataillone (improvised infantry battalions), Pionier-Ersatz- und-Ausbildungs-Bataillon 68, Landes-Pionier-Bataillon 513, Bewährungs- Bataillon z.b.V. 500 (a probation unit), two Volkssturm units, a battalion of Hungarian troops, four battalions of Hilfswillige[6] and a number of other Kampfgruppen and smaller units.

6. Eastern European auxiliary troops

two rivers, was founded in the 13th century, close to an already-existing Slavic settlement. Its importance rose after a permanent bridge was erected over the Oder. In the 14th century a castle was built and in the 16th century the settlement was turned into a fortress town, being surrounded by walls with bastions and gates. The constant growth of the population soon forced the inhabitants to settle outside the city and suburbs sprang up on the far sides of both rivers. West of the Oder were the settlements of Küstrin-Kietz and Kuhbrücken-Vorstadt; east of the Warthe lay what would become the Neustadt.

The 17th century brought further modifications of the town's fortifications, a bridgehead bastion being built on the Oder-Insel (the island lying immediately to the west and across from the Altstadt, between the main course of the river and its western arm, the Vorflut-Kanal) and additional bastions on the east side of town. However, these did not prevent destruction of the town by the Russian army in 1758. In 1806 the fortress was captured by the Napoleonic French army, only to be recaptured by the Prussians in 1814.

During the Industrial Revolution, Küstrin lost much of its importance. However, its fortifications were maintained and still new forts and outworks were created at the end of the century. All except one were built on the east bank of the Warthe within a radius of five to ten kilometres from the old fortress. Already outdated during their construction, they were no longer useful in modern warfare. Meanwhile, the constant growth of the suburb on the east side of the Warthe led to its development into a separate modern city district – the Neustadt (New Town) – much larger in area than the Altstadt.

By the beginning of the 20th century, Küstrin was still a communications hub. Two main roads, including Reichsstrasse 1, the Berlin–Königsberg highway, and two main railway lines passed through the city, carried across the rivers by five bridges: a road and railway bridge across the Oder and a road and two railway bridges across the Warthe.

Even though by 1945 only a fortress in name, the city still housed a considerable garrison and featured three military barracks: the Infanterie-Kaserne 'Von Stulpnagel' and the Pionier-Klinke-Kaserne, both located in the eastern half of the Neustadt, and the Artillerie-Kaserne on the Oder Island.

Part III. Festung Küstrin • 113

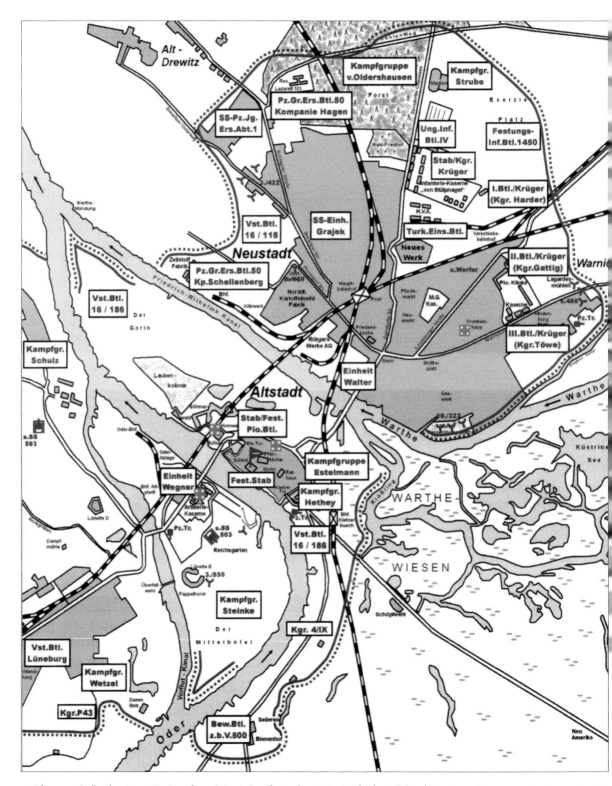

This map of Küstrin shows the location of the defending units at the beginning of the siege. (Der Krieg An Der Oder. Ein Tagebuch)

The defence of Küstrin was supposed to be strengthened by twelve so-called Panthertürme, which were tank turrets of PzKpfw V complete with its powerful 75mm gun but set up in fixed positions. They were to be operated by personnel of Festungs-Pantherturm-Kompanie 1211. However, only five of the twelve turrets managed to reach the fortress, the other seven falling into Soviet hands east of Küstrin. Here, men of Kampfgruppe Hethey, the infantry unit defending the southern entrance to the Altstadt, pose at the emplacement prepared for the Pantherturm on Kietzer Strasse, the main road leading to the Altstadt from the south-east. In anticipation of its completion the turret has been placed beside it on a temporary base. The fortification visible in the background is Bastion Philipp. (Hans Greiser)

Kietzer Strasse is today named Ulica Chyzanska. No visible signs of the turret emplacement remain but, with the wooden hut gone, one now has a clearer view of the bastion. The Kietz Gate lies just around the corner on the right. (Tomasz Zgoda)

Artillery support was provided by Artillerie-Ersatz-Abteilung 39, Flak-Regiment 114, and a Nebelwerfer-Batterie. In all, the fortress fielded around 105 guns, including at least twenty-four 10.5cm heavy and twenty-four light Flak guns, plus eighteen 7.5cm PaK 40 anti-tank guns.

Although the fortress area was quite small, it had its own armoured unit, consisting of three Königstiger tanks from schwere SS-Panzer-Abteilung 503, five fixed Panther turrets from Festungs-Pantherturm-Kompanie 1211 and at least one Hetzer tank destroyer.

Most of these forces were concentrated in the Neustadt. With its compact buildings and industrial areas, it was particularly suited for prolonged defence. The Altstadt, situated as it was between the Warthe and Oder, with

Part III. Festung Küstrin • 115

The same emplacement but now looking the other way, across Kietzer Strasse and towards the Ravelin August-Wilhelm. (A ravelin is a triangular fortification or detached outwork located in front of the innerworks of a fortress). This particular Pantherturm was disabled on 27th March by a direct artillery hit on the barrel. Of the other four Panthertürme, one was set up on the Oder Island just east of the Vorflut-Kanal road bridge to cover the western approaches (Reichsstrasse 1); two were emplaced in Lagardesmühlen to cover the eastern approaches (Warnicker Strasse), and the last one was probably also on the Island, near the Altstadt railway station. (Hans Greiser)

Ravelin August-Wilhelm still bears the scars of Soviet shelling. (Tomasz Zgoda)

land access only via a single road from the south, was easily defendable too. However, most of its buildings were to some degree of wooden construction and thus a fire risk, and its old casemates were not designed to protect against modern bombs and artillery. Advantageous for the defence were the extensive water meadows of the Warthe that stretched out immediately east of the Altstadt. Deliberate flooding had not only inundated these areas but also the whole Warthe estuary to the south-east, forming an additional protective obstruction against approach from that direction.

Frantically, the city prepared for defence. Soldiers and civilians were mobilised to build trenches, fieldworks and anti-tank obstacles. However, the ground was hard-frozen and so digging of trenches and anti-tank ditches initially proved virtually impossible and the defenders were forced to continue construction of fortifications well into the siege. All in all, two defensive lines were created consisting of trenches with barbed wire and roadblocks. In the Neustadt, the Infantry and Engineers Barracks, the Neues Werk fort and the Cellulose Factory were prepared for prolonged defence. On the east bank of the Oder, the Bienenhof inn (two kilometres south of the Altstadt on the Göritz road) and the pumping-station, on the main road to the south-east, were manned and turned into strong points. Likewise, on the river's west bank, the Dammmeisterei (lock keeper's house) and the Konradshof and Weinbergshof inns at the Kietz suburb were made into fortified outposts. All the bridges over the Oder, the Warthe and the Vorflut-Kanal were prepared for demolition.

All these preparations were offset by the fact that, in the days after Küstrin was declared a fortress, the Red Army had already crossed the Oder and established footholds on both sides of the city. Fifteen kilometres to the north, the 5th Shock Army under Lieutenant-General Nikolai Berzarin gained a small bridgehead near the village of Kienitz on 31st January. The crossing was first established by the 283rd Guards Rifle Regiment of the 94th Guards Rifle Division. Nine kilometres south of the city, the 8th Guards Army under Colonel-General Vasily Chuikov did the same near the village of Reitwein, Here, the 47th and 79th Guards Rifle Divisions created three small bridgeheads on 2nd February. The danger of a complete encirclement of the city now loomed large. To make matters worse, the Soviets, under the cover of the thickly forested woodland, occupied the hills north of the Neustadt which provided them with good observation of the German defences.

FIRST CONTACT

Elements of the Soviet 1st Mechanised Corps (Lieutenant-General Semen Krivoshein) arrived in the area north of Küstrin on 31st January. They quickly took the undefended villages of Kalenzig, Alt Schaumburg and Alt Drewitz, in the process liberating the nearby Stalag 3 prisoner-of-war camp.

That same afternoon, tanks and infantry from the 219th Armoured Brigade, 19th Mechanised Brigade and 57th Motorcycle Battalion launched a surprise attack on the Neustadt from different directions. A few tanks managed to penetrate to within 400 metres of the Warthe road bridge to the Altstadt. However, they were forced to change direction due to the mass of refugee vehicles that jammed the streets in vain attempts to cross the river.

Recovering from the initial shock, and despite their basic lack of arms and ammunition, the German defenders managed to repulse the Soviet attacks. Soldiers from Panzergrenadier-Ersatz-Bataillon 50 and from the I. Abteilung of Artillery-Regiment 25 (a unit of the 25. Panzergrenadier-Division that had just arrived by train) knocked out at least three tanks with Panzerfausts and

On 31st January, the Soviets made their first incursion into the city, a force of tanks and infantry penetrating into the Neustadt aiming for the Warthe bridges. The force employed was not strong enough and its route was blocked by refugees crowding the roads. Several of the tanks were knocked out during their push. This Valentine Mk IX of the 57th Motorcycle Battalion was disabled by a Panzerfaust on Plantagen-Strasse. Most of the crew managed to get out, only to be captured in a garden area of the nearby Rütgers-Werke works by a detachment under Oberleutnant Erich Bölke. The tank's gunner had been killed as he was about to push the trigger of the main 6-pounder gun. His corpse must have slowly slumped forward because a few days later the gun suddenly fired, tearing a hole in the wall of a first-storey living room across the street! British and Canadian-produced Valentines were supplied in large numbers to the Soviet Union under Lend-Lease. (Horst Wewetzer)

Plantagen-Strasse is today named Ulica Niepodleglosci. The buildings on the eastern side of the street have all been cleared away but those on the opposite side largely remain. (Tomasz Zgoda)

killed several dozen Soviet soldiers. Further Russian attacks, now supported by an artillery barrage from SU-152 assault guns of the 347th Guards Heavy Assault Gun Regiment, did not succeed either. These initial attacks, in essence nothing more than a reconnaissance in force, failed because the forces employed were too small and their actions uncoordinated.

The following day, 1st February, the Soviets captured the Cellulose Factory strong point by the Warthe river. The surviving defenders, a platoon from Küstrin's Volkssturm-Bataillon 16/186, were shot as 'partisans', prompting Kreisleiter Körner to issue all his Volkssturm troops with uniforms and pay books.

On 2nd February, the 32nd Rifle Corps, part of the 5th Shock Army and

This Sherman M4A2 (76)W of the 219th Armoured Brigade was knocked out by a Panzerfaust at the railway underpass on Plantagen-Strasse – it can be seen in the background of the picture opposite. Note the makeshift winter camouflage made up from bedsheets. The Cyrillic 'L' with a dot inside visible on the turret is the emblem of the I Mechanised Corps to which the brigade belonged. The Panzerfaust was fired from the railway embankment and penetrated the rear of the turret, killing the entire crew. The escorting infantry seated on the deck were thrown off by the explosion and were all mown down. One of them can be seen lying behind the tank. (Horst Wewetzer)

Another shot of the Sherman but now looking the other way. Some of the Soviet tanks were destroyed as they tried to retreat out of the city, which explains why the Sherman – and the Valentine seen earlier – are not facing towards the bridges but to the north, back from whence they had come. As can be seen here, the Germans later cleverly incorporated the tank into a roadblock, closing the rest of the underpass with wooden beams. (Eiermann)

The viaduct carries the Szczecin (Stettin) to Wroclaw (Breslau) railway line, and the former Hauptbahnhof (main railway station) is just a few hundred metres away to the left. (Tomasz Zgoda)

Part III. Festung Küstrin • 119

From 2nd February, the defence of Küstrin was led by SS-Gruppenführer Heinz Reinefarth. He initially had his command post in the Kommandantur (garrison headquarters building) in the Altstadt but when this was destroyed a few days later, it was moved to the nearby Schloss (castle). Here, Reinefarth and his adjutant, SS-Sturmbannführer Siegfried Hoffmann, are seen leaving a cellar located in the castle's entrance wing. (BA Bild 183-R97892)

The 1945 battles left the Altstadt in such a state of destruction that the Polish authorities (Küstrin having become a Polish border city as a result of the Yalta Conference) decided to completely clear away the ruins, utilising much of the re-usable material in the reconstruction of Warsaw. The last vestiges were razed in 1967, leaving virtually nothing except the Festung's old fortifications. For over two decades, the area was a forbidden zone and it was not until after the fall of the Iron Curtain in 1989 that the old street grid and some of the foundations of former buildings – the Schloss, the Pfarrkirche, etc – were laid bare again. Of the castle, only its foundations and basements remain today. This is looking east from the former courtyard. (Tomasz Zgoda)

commanded by Major-General Dmitri Sherebin, arrived in the Küstrin area with three divisions. The 60th Guards Rifle Division (Major-General Vasily Pavlovich Sokolov) reinforced the Oder bridgehead at Kienitz north of the city, the 295th Rifle Division (Major-General Alexander Petrovich Dorofeev) occupied positions north of the Neustadt and the 416th Rifle Division (Major-General Dmitry Mikhailovich) east of it. They were ordered to capture the city and enlarge the bridgehead north of it to a line running from the town of Letschin (west of Kienitz) south-east via the villages of Zechin, Genschmar and Alt Bleyen back to Küstrin. However, stiff German resistance and insufficient forces made this order impossible to fulfil. Worse still, under concerted counter-attack, the 295th Rifle Division lost the Cellulose Factory.

The same day, after having been Fortress Commander for just a week,

An infantry patrol passing a road barricade on Kurze-Damm-Strasse in the Altstadt on their way towards the Neustadt in early March. Later on, the road-block was closed by a double-decker Berlin bus filled with rubble (the bus had brought Flak personnel to Küstrin in January). The smoke seen rising in the distance is from the area of the Norddeutsche Kartoffelmehl-Fabrik (North-German Potato-Flower Factory), one of the German strong points in the defence of the Neustadt. Note the rubble lying in the street – evidence that the city has been under Soviet artillery fire for some time. (Mahn- Und Gedenkstätte Seelower Höhen)

Kurze-Damm-Strasse is now named Ulica Jana z Kostrzyna. The three buildings seen here are a belated attempt at rebuilding the layout of the Old Town. (Tomasz Zgoda)

122 • RED ARMY TOWARDS THE ODER – THEN AND NOW

Generalmajor Raegener was relieved of his command and replaced by SS-Gruppenführer Heinz Reinefarth. Known as 'the Butcher of Warsaw' for his brutal suppression of the Warsaw Uprising in August-September 1944, Reinefarth had a fearsome reputation. He had been awarded the Knight's Cross in 1942 and had held a string of senior positions in the Waffen-SS, Ordnungspolizei and as the Police Chief in the Wartheland. Hitler put Reinefarth in command of Küstrin to ensure execution of his order to hold the city to the last man. By this point of the war, the Führer had all but lost faith in the officers of the Wehrmacht – in no small way as a consequence of the 20th July 1944 bomb plot. Instead, he relied increasingly on die-hard fanatical SS commanders.

Dividing the Festung into two sectors, Reinefarth in his turn appointed Oberst Franz Walter as commander of the Neustadt. This was a strange choice as the latter was a colonel in the Feldgendarmerie without any military experience. Command of the Altstadt was given to Major Otto Wegner.

Meanwhile, fighting had also broken out on the southern approaches to the Altstadt. On 3rd February, Mikhailovich's 416th Rifle Division was able to capture the pumping-station, just a kilometre south-east of the Altstadt, and turn it into a strong point. From there the Soviets were able to shell the Altstadt. However, the Bienenhof inn, staunchly defended by men of Bewährungs-Bataillon z.b.V. 500, remained in German hands, preventing the Soviets from approaching the Altstadt from that direction. It would remain a highly-contested position until the very last days of the siege.

The Soviet failure to capture the city in late January and through February could be blamed on several factors. First of all, even the Soviet command was surprised by the speed of their advance through Poland and lacked comprehensive intelligence of the enemy's strength and defences around the town. The German garrison, though small and ill equipped, was strong enough to repulse the initial forays aimed at capturing the city. Moreover, the Soviet forces arrived piecemeal, weakened by two weeks of fighting through Poland and were thrown into the attack without planning and without logistical support, which lagged far behind.

Secondly, the two armies in the Küstrin area – Berzarin's 5th Shock Army (assigned to capture the Neustadt and the Altstadt) and Chuikov's 8th Guards Army (tasked with taking Küstrin-Kietz) – were separated from each other by the fortress and the Oder. This led to their attacks being poorly co-ordinated, enabling the Germans to keep them at bay for two months.

Thirdly, Marshall Zhukov's final offensive – the attack on Berlin – as initially planned was to be launched from the bridgehead near Frankfurt-an-der-Oder, thirty kilometres to the south, hence breaking the German defences around Küstrin was not initially a priority for him. It only became so when Stalin brought the final date of the Berlin offensive forward. By that time, Zhukov had no other choice but to start his offensive from the bridgeheads west of Küstrin, the area closest to Berlin, so taking that stronghold suddenly became an essential prerequisite.

German soldiers passing a number of captured ex-French M1917 155mm guns discarded and dumped by the side of the road, probably due to lack of ammunition. They are on Adolf-Hitler-Strasse, the street running from the Altstadt across the Warthe bridge into the Neustadt, near the railway crossing just north of the Altstadt. The east side of the street has been covered with a sheet screen in order to prevent the enemy from observing German movements.
(BA Bild 146-1971-033-41)

Today this street is named Ulica Sikorskiego. The view is north, towards the Warthe bridge. The tram tracks have been removed, though the rail crossing remains.
(Tomasz Zgoda)

STALEMATE

During the first month of the siege, the 32nd Rifle Corps held back from any major assaults on the fortress. One of the very few attacks occurred on 12th February, when the 295th Rifle Division tried in vain to pierce the German defences along Zorndorfer Chaussee, the main road leading into the Neustadt from the north.

For the remainder of February, the front line in the Neustadt remained static, running in a semicircle around the built-up area. Seen clockwise from west to east, it began at the Cellulose Factory on the bank of the Warthe, running generally north past Alt Drewitz village (in Russian hands), then curving eastwards to follow the line of the Kohlenweg until the latter's crossroads with Zorndorfer Chaussee, where it curved south-eastwards to run across the Exerzier-Platz (drill-ground) of the infantry barracks and across the Verschiebe-Bahnhof (goods station) railway junction to the Lagardesmühlen housing estate, before reaching the west bank of the Jungfern-Kanal, which then led back to the Warthe.

German forces defending the Neustadt were distributed as follows. The western half of the line was held by Panzergrenadier-Ersatz-Bataillon 50, Volkssturm-Bataillon 16/115 and SS-Panzerjäger-Ersatz-Abteilung 1. The northern frontage along the Kohlenweg and Exerzier-Platz was manned by Kampfgruppe von Oldershausen and Kampfgruppe Strube. The eastern sector was occupied by Festungs-Infanterie-Bataillon 1450 and Kampfgruppe Krüger (a regimental-size unit commanded by Oberst Rudolf Krüger and comprising three battalions). Stationed as back-up units near the infantry barracks were the Hungarian Bataillon 89/IV and one of the Turkoman auxiliary battalions. Securing the three Warthe bridges was a unit known as Einheit Walter.

Defending the Altstadt were Kampfgruppen Estelmann and Hethey and Volkssturm-Bataillon 16/186. Also in the Old Town, based at the castle, was Reinefarth's Festungs-Stab (fortress command staff). The southern approaches to the Altstadt were covered by Bewährungs-Bataillon z.b.V. 500 and Kampfgruppe 4/IX. The Oder Island was defended by Einheit Wegner and Kampfgruppe Steinke.

While most of the soldiers manned the defences as ordered, some of them abandoned their posts and went plundering nearby buildings looking to improve their meagre food rations; others deserted and sought to hide themselves, hoping they may avoid the fight and being caught by their own side. Those apprehended faced summary judgment and were promptly shot or publicly hanged.

Life in the besieged city was extremely hard for the 8,000 to 10,000 civilians who had remained. The Soviet shelling formed a constant threat. Fires raging throughout the city and damage to buildings deprived many of proper shelter. After the destruction of the gasworks and fuel tanks, heating of buildings was impossible. Many survived only thanks to the mild winter

conditions. By the end of February, the water supply was also running out and a canteen was set up for those unable to feed themselves. The old fortifications and two schools in the Altstadt were turned into hospitals.

Evacuation of the civilians was first allowed on 4th February, but soon halted due to a lack of transport. It was not resumed until 19th February and completed a week later. However, hundreds of civilians – members of the Volkssturm, physicians, nurses, firemen, officials and various workers – stayed in the city to help defend it and keep it functioning.

On 19th February, a stray shell hit one of the demolition chambers of the Warthe road bridge, causing it to explode and collapsing one of its spans. After provisional repair it was negotiable only by pedestrians, vehicles being forced to use the nearby railway bridge. The collapse of the road bridge also severed the water mains to the Altstadt, leaving the inhabitants with only the old street-pumps for their water supply.

FALL OF THE NEUSTADT

After the two weeks of respite, General Berzarin, the 5th Shock Army commander, ordered Sherebin's 32nd Rifle Corps, with the 295th and 416th Rifle Divisions, to capture both the Neustadt and Altstadt by 28th February. However, the armour and artillery assigned to support this attack were

A 2cm Flak 30/38 Flakvierling emplaced near the Hafen, the river harbour located on the south bank of the Warthe just west of the easternmost railway bridge. The picture was taken on 7th March, the first day of the Soviet offensive on the Neustadt. Smoke rises from fires across the river and visible in the distance are the chimneys of the heavily-embattled Norddeutsche Kartoffelmehl-Fabrik. (BA Bild 146-1990-060-02)

Nature has reclaimed most of this once industrial area.
(Tomasz Zgoda)

unable to concentrate in time, so the starting date had to be postponed to 6th March.

The corps assault plan called for Dorofeev's 295th Rifle Division to launch the main attack on the Neustadt from the north-west, striking with two regiments concentrated on the front between the Warthe and the Berlin-to-Stettin railway line. On the right, the 1038th Rifle Regiment (minus its 2nd Battalion) – supported by two IS-2 tanks from the 89th Guards Tank Regiment, four T-34 tanks from the 92nd Engineer Tank Regiment and an engineer company – was to recapture the Cellulose Factory along with other factories situated on the river bank. Once they were taken, it was to clear its side of the Neustadt of German resistance. On the left, the 1040th Rifle Regiment, supported by five IS-2 and ten T-34 tanks from the same armoured units and two engineer companies, was to attack and capture the Infantry Barracks, then take the area of the Hauptbahnhof, and later on clear its sector of the city. After securing the Neustadt, both regiments were to take up positions along the Warthe riverbank. Further east, the division's third regiment, the 1042nd Rifle Regiment, holding the line from the Berlin-to-Stettin railway line to the Jungfern-Kanal, was to carry out an amphibious landing along the canal to gain a foothold in the southern part of the Neustadt in the area of the gasworks. In addition, three penal companies were ordered to attack towards the Engineers Barracks.

Left: Another quadruple 2cm gun on the bank of the Warthe river, this one emplaced immediately east of the access road (Adolf-Hitler-Strasse) to the road bridge — more signs of the sheet screen erected along the street on the left. Visible in the background is the Neustadt after it was hit by Katyusha rocket launchers on 7th February. In all, the garrison fielded twenty-four 2cm Flak guns, mostly operated by men from leichte Flak-Abteilung 850 and two separate batteries, leichte Flak-Batterien z.b.V. 6522 and 10284.

No traces of the gun pit can be discerned today and, here too, dense vegetation obscures the view towards the Neustadt. (Tomasz Zgoda)

The corps' other formation, Mikhailovich's 416th Rifle Division, was to hold itself ready to support the 295th Rifle Division in their efforts to take the Neustadt, and later the Altstadt and the Oder-Insel.

The assault was to be supported by air strikes provided by the 16th Air Army and an artillery barrage from ten artillery regiments and a Katyusha rocket-launcher regiment. Further support was to come from a regiment each of tanks and heavy tanks, a flame-thrower battalion and an engineer battalion. This support was badly needed to establish Soviet numerical superiority over the Germans as at that point it was only 1.5 to 1 – a ratio far below what was usual to have any confidence of success. To increase their effectiveness, the Soviet infantry was organised into assault groups consisting of small teams equipped with flame-throwers, explosives and captured Panzerfausts, and supported by artillery and tanks.

In order to confuse the Germans as to where the main assault would come, the Soviets ostentatiously shifted infantry units and artillery in areas visible to the enemy and drove armoured vehicles close to the front line in the sector occupied by the 1042nd Rifle Regiment.

Starting on 26th February, the 16th Air Army increased its presence in the area, bombing and strafing German positions and important facilities in the fortress. Many buildings on the east bank of the Warthe, among them several factories, were set ablaze. The German fire services had great difficulty putting out the conflagrations due to shortages of manpower and lack of equipment.

The Soviet assault started before dawn on 6th March. At 0400-hrs twelve boats carrying sixty men of the 1042nd Rifle Regiment came down the Jungfern-Kanal, attempting to land on the southern shore of the Neustadt.

Another shot of the Sherman pictured on page 119 but now taken during the final Russian attack to capture the Neustadt, which began on 7th March. The Soviet infantrymen, most likely belonging to the 295th Rifle Division, are advancing towards the Stern, the main road junction in the Neustadt. (Marek Wichrowski via Muzeum Twierdzy Kostrzyn)

Looking north-west up Ulica Niepodleglosci in 2019. (Tomasz Zgoda)

130 • RED ARMY TOWARDS THE ODER – THEN AND NOW

However, they were spotted and fired on by machine guns and light anti-aircraft guns. After losing two boats the attack was abandoned. Then, at 0620-hrs the three penal companies attacked towards the Engineers Barracks. They too were greeted with overwhelming fire, including missiles fired by the Festung's Nebelwerfer battery, and their assault failed as well. Nevertheless, these two actions drew German attention away from the north-western sector of the front line where the main attack was to be launched.

Heavy cloud cover precluded the air support that had been planned for this assault and a decision was taken to postpone it until the following day. However, this decision failed to be communicated to the neighbouring 8th Guards Army, on the other side of the Oder, which launched its attack on Kietz as originally planned.

The second day of the 32nd Rifle Corps' operation began at 1030-hrs, again with an attack staged by 1042nd Rifle Regiment, much as it had done the previous day. Its 3rd Battalion and the three penal companies struck parallel to the Berlin–Königsberg railway line. After an hour of fighting they occupied the first German trench line and soon fierce fighting was raging for the gasworks. However, German resistance stiffened and the Soviet troops were pushed back towards the first line of German trenches.

At 1100-hrs the Soviet main attack began. It opened with a massive artillery and aerial bombardment of the German defence lines in the Neustadt. For about two hours 142 bombers, escorted by 85 fighters, bombed and strafed the German positions. The defenders shot down four aircraft but could not prevent the bombers from destroying their artillery positions and trench lines. Immediately following the artillery barrage troops of the 1038th and 1040th Rifle Regiments moved forward covered by a smoke-screen from 4,500 smoke canisters, At first, the assault proceeded as planned, the stunned and battered defenders unable to mount any significant resistance. Their only success, though short lived, was the recapture of Reserve-Lazarett 101, the military hospital along Kohlenweg in the north-west corner of the Neustadt. By 1400-hrs. the two Soviet regiments had pierced the German perimeter defences in three places and advanced a kilometre into the Neustadt. As they moved into the urban area, their advance slowed. At 1500-hrs. the Soviets attacked in the area of the Infantry Barracks. By now the Germans had been pushed back to a line running from the Warthe to a point on the Berlin–Stettin railway line around 350 metres north-east of the Hauptbahnhof.

Hoping to reinforce success, General Sherebin, the 32nd Rifle Corps commander, now decided to commit the 416th Rifle Division. Supported by a howitzer regiment, two mortar regiments and a couple of tanks, it was instructed to capture the south-eastern part of the Neustadt. In connection with this, the 295th Rifle Division had its orders changed. Its 1038th Rifle Regiment was now to capture the northernmost railway bridge over the Warthe and the 1040th Rifle Regiment to crush the enemy defences around

This furniture lorry had been used as transport by the crew of a 12cm mortar but was badly hit at the very start of the battle. Notwithstanding the destruction of its cabin, it remained roadworthy. The picture was taken on Friedrich-Strasse, beside the Ravelin Christian-Ludwig, on the north-western side of the Altstadt. Inside the ravelin was the Jugendherberge 'Markgraf Johann', the local youth hostel run by the Hitlerjugend. A public air raid shelter in the hostel grounds was taken into use as a front-line cinema during the siege. On 22nd March, during one of its screenings, the ravelin was hit by three heavy Soviet bombs, causing numerous casualties in the cinema. (Horst Wewetzer)

The ravelin was demolished after the war and no trace of it remains along what is today Ulica Graniczna, its place taken by a Polish currency exchange office. (Tomasz Zgoda)

the Hauptbahnhof whilst simultaneously linking up with the 1042nd Rifle Regiment advancing from the north. However, the new forces were stopped 500 metres west and north of the railway station.

During the night of 7th/8th March, Reinefarth ordered an all-out counter-attack on the advancing Soviets. At 0345-hrs German forces moved out from the Neues Werk fort and the Hauptbahnhof as well as from the Norddeutsche Kartoffelmehl-Fabrik[7] on the Warthe riverbank. At first the attack looked promising but it soon came to a standstill. Realising his forces were too weak to push the enemy back, Reinefarth issued orders to hold the two bridgeheads defending the Warthe bridges.

On this second day, Sherebin's two divisions had advanced as much as two kilometres into the German defences on a frontage of two and a half kilometres but they had failed to capture the Warthe bridges or separate the defenders of the Neustadt from the Altstadt. Once again, insufficient forces and lack of powerful artillery pieces were the reasons given for this disappointing result.

For the third day of the attack, 8th March, the 295th Rifle Division ordered its 1038th Rifle Regiment to capture three factories along the Warthe riverbank and sever the Neustadt from the Altstadt. The 1040th and 1042nd Rifle Regiments were meanwhile to take the eastern and north-eastern parts of the Neustadt, and the 416th Rifle Division the centre.

The attack opened at 0700-hrs with a ten-minute artillery barrage. On the heels of this, the Soviet assault groups moved forward. During the day, Soviet aircraft flew around 200 sorties in support of the attacks. Advances were made towards the main railway station, the Friedenskirche church and the gasworks. The Germans launched multiple counter-attacks but each time were forced back. However, their resistance was such that the 1038th Rifle Regiment failed in its task to capture the factories along the river. By the end of the day the regiment, with the help of the 416th Rifle Division's 1368th Rifle Regiment, had closed up on the two small German bridgeheads defending the Warthe bridges.

The other two regiments of the 295th Rifle Division achieved better results. The 1040th Rifle Regiment, after some fierce fighting, captured the main railway station. After this success, it was ordered to attack towards the Engineers Barracks, link up with the 1042nd Rifle Regiment and thus cut off and isolate a large part of the German forces in the Neustadt. That evening, the 1040th Regiment, together with the 416th Rifle Division's 1374th Rifle Regiment, reached the area of the Berlin–Königsberg railway and the sawmill, severing these forces' last connection with the Altstadt.

Thus by the end of the day, as the Neustadt burned, a large part of the German forces had been driven back into two isolated pockets. One pocket encompassed the area of the Infantry Barracks and Neues Werk and was composed of what remained of Kampfgruppen von Oldershausen and Strube, Festungs-Infanterie-Bataillon 1450 and the I. Bataillon of Kampfgruppe Krüger. The second formed up around the Engineers

---

7. North-German Potato-Flower Factory

German soldiers entering Bastion Philipp, the old fortification at the south-western corner of the Altstadt, in early February. Fortress casemates offered some protection from the Soviet shelling for the German troops manning the Altstadt. (Gerd Körner)

Bastion Philipp has been restored in recent years and today houses a Fortress Museum with a permanent exhibition on the history of the city. The concrete construction that covered the entrance in 1945 has been removed. (Tomasz Zgoda)

Barracks and the Lagardesmühlen housing estate and comprised the other two battalions of Kampfgruppe Krüger.

At 2300-hrs that night, Reinefarth ordered the last two bridges remaining over the Warthe to be blown.

The following day, 9th March, the 1038th Rifle Regiment finally recaptured the Cellulose Factory. It had been defended to the end by a company from Panzergrenadier-Ersatz-Bataillon 50. Three other factories along the riverbank also fell to the Soviets. The 416th Rifle Division, in co-operation with the other regiments of the 295th Rifle Division, cleared the southern part of the Neustadt and finally cleared the gasworks. These forces were then sent north in order to help destroy the two pockets of resistance holding out in the Neustadt.

On 10th and 11th March the 2nd Battalion of the 1038 Rifle Regiment and the 1st and 2nd Battalions of the 1368th Rifle Regiment established small footholds on the west bank of the Warthe. However, lack of artillery support and the fact that most of the Soviet forces were still occupied with mopping up the Neustadt forced them to withdraw.

During the night of 11th/12th March the German force, who remained cooped up in the Neues Werk and Infantry Barracks pocket, tried to break out from its encirclement. Just a few soldiers managed to fight their way out, only to be captured in the city forest just to the north or near the village of Tamsel, four kilometres to the north-east. This final attempt to avoid captivity coincided with the Soviet assault on this last enemy hold-out in the Neustadt. Only a few individual soldiers managed to escape, cross the Oder north of Küstrin, and reach their own lines.

That day, Colonel-General Mikhail Malinin, the Chief-of-Staff of the First Byelorussian Front, informed Stalin that Küstrin had been captured. This was of course premature and incorrect as the Altstadt and Kietz were still in German hands. However, it was too late to correct the news. Stalin had already ordered a 12-salvo salute by 124 guns in Moscow to celebrate the feat, and media all over the world announced that the Soviets had captured the last fortress before Berlin. This left Marshal Zhukov with no other choice but to quickly capture the remaining parts of the city.

ENVELOPMENT

As the battle for Festung Küstrin unfolded, it was vital for the defenders that its lines of communications to the rear were kept open. With the Russians already having gained bridgeheads both north and south of the city in late January to early February, there was a real danger that these would join up and thus surround the Festung, severing its access and supply route.

Responsibility for holding the sector of the Oder of which Küstrin formed a part fell to German 9. Armee, commanded by General der Infanterie Theodor Busse. By early February it had begun taking over defence of the river line with four infantry divisions, (three of them newly-raised and

The railway bridge over the Oder linking the Altstadt with the Oder-Insel (Oder Island), seen from the Alstadt side. Note the machine-gun dugout on the far left and the sentries on the bridge. The soldier in the centre is gathering wood. This bridge would end up as the last remaining bridge over the Oder, and be used in the chaotic evacuation of the Altstadt garrison, being blown by German engineers in the evening of 28th March — but with a sizable number of retreating soldiers still on it. (Horst Wewetzer)

It was rebuilt in 1947 (using parts of the blown Karnin lift bridge on the Ducherow–Swinemünde railway line) but until 1992 was only used for Soviet military train transports. Today the Oder forms the border between Germany and Poland. (Johannes Bönisch)

incomplete), plus a panzer division freshly transferred from the Western front. From north to south were Infanterie-Division 303 'Döberitz', Infanterie-Division 309 'Berlin', the 21. Panzer-Division, Panzergrenadier-Division 'Kurmark' and the 712. Infanterie-Division. The panzer division was placed immediately west of Küstrin as a mobile 'fire brigade'.

The part of Küstrin that lay west of the Oder was defended by two of the garrison's own formations: the Kietz suburb, located on Reichsstrasse 1, was defended by Kampfgruppe Wetzel, and Kuhbrücken-Vorstadt, a tiny hamlet nestling in a hollow surrounded by dykes two kilometres to the north, was held by Kampfgruppe Schulz. The Kampfgruppe's position linked in with those of the 9. Armee's divisions on either flank.

The Oder road bridge, located just south of the railway bridge, was partially shattered by a direct hit from a Soviet bomb on the night of 25th/26th March. Here the two wrecked bridges (the road bridge in front) are seen from the Altstadt side of the river. On the right stands the ruin of Küstrin's castle. (Camo)

Just one day after gaining its bridgeheads south of the city, the 8th Guards Army had already began its outward expansion. On 3rd February, the 47th Guards Rifle Division (Major-General Vasily Mikhailovich Shugayev), supported by two regiments of the 416th Rifle Division, captured the villages of Manschnow and Neu Manschnow as well as many nearby farmsteads, and succeeded in cutting Reichsstrasse 1 and the Berlin-Küstrin railway line at a point west of Kietz. Road and rail communications with Küstrin were now severed.

Reacting quickly to this setback, 9. Armee immediately sought to restore the connection to the fortress, sending in the 21. Panzer-Division (Oberst Helmut Zollenkopf). Its first attack, launched on 7th February, failed but after two days of further fighting the road link with the fortress was re-established. The following day, 10th February, the 21. Panzer-Division went into 9. Armee reserve, being replaced by the 25. Panzergrenadier-Division (Generalmajor Arnold Burmeister).

The bridges — unlike the castle — were rebuilt after the war. (Tomasz Zgoda)

Part III. Festung Küstrin • 137

Four days later, on 14th February, the 35th Guards Rifle Division (Colonel Nikolai Nikolaevich Zaiolyev) was ordered to capture Kietz. However, their advance was halted by the difficult terrain – the whole area was muddy agricultural land that greatly hindered the movement of heavy vehicles. The German defenders were strongly backed by Flak artillery being used in a ground role, which repulsed all Soviet tank attacks, whether it was being used en-mass or in support of infantry attacks.

After these initial skirmishes, the fighting in this area subsided and stalemate set in. For a full three weeks the front west of the Oder remained an edgy stand-off.

On 6th March – the day on which the 5th Shock Army on the other side of the Warthe had been supposed to launch its attack on the Neustadt – the 8th Guards Army renewed its attack on Kietz with a view to once again cutting off the fortress. Following a two-and-a-half-hour artillery barrage, Zaiolyev's 35th and Shugayev's 47th Guards Rifle Divisions struck but the first day's fighting did not result in them gaining any significant territory. Both sides fought fiercely and it was not until the evening of 8th March that the Russians succeeded in taking the Kietz railway station. Over the next few days they managed to force their way to within 300 metres of the Vorflut-Kanal bridges to the Oder Island and capture almost the entire German bridgehead. By the 13th the Germans had been forced to give up the Dammmeisterei strong point.

However, although most of Kietz was now lost, the Germans succeeded in keeping a narrow line of communications with the besieged fortress open. It followed Reichsstrasse 1 to a point west of Manschnow, then turned off the highway northwards to the town of Golzow, where it swung east to follow a minor road to the village of Gorgast. From here, it turned north-eastwards, following a back road that ran past the Alt Bleyen manor farm and then south to Kuhbrücken-Vorstadt before re-joining Reichsstrasse 1, just short of the railway bridge across the Vorflut-Kanal and into Küstrin. The road bridge had been made impassable by an artillery hit on 5th March.

Six kilometres long and just two kilometres wide, sandwiched between Soviet positions to the north and south, this narrow corridor was known to the Germans as the Schlauch-Stellung (pipeline position). It was a vital access and supply line, allowing nightly transports of reinforcements, ammunition, supplies and mail into the fortress and the evacuation of civilians, wounded soldiers and unneeded supplies out of it. The 25. Panzergrenadier-Division was tasked with keeping it open.

On 13th March, having finally reduced the Neustadt, Marshal Zhukov issued new orders for the unification of the bridgeheads north and south of Küstrin and the final encirclement of the enemy fortress. The 5th Shock Army in the north was instructed to use two reinforced divisions of the 32nd Rifle Corps – the 60th Guards Rifle Division and the 295th Rifle Division – in a main attack towards Golzow. The 1373rd Rifle Regiment of the 416th Rifle Division was to make a secondary thrust towards Gorgast. The 8th

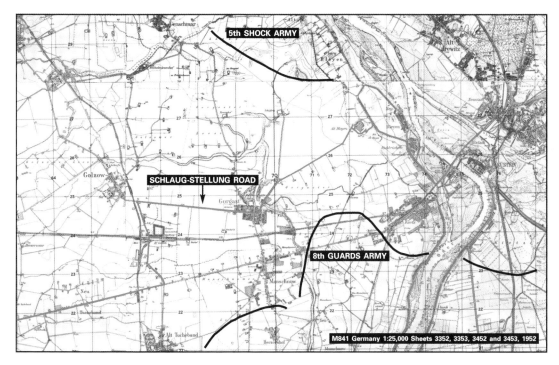

Map showing the area to the west of Küstrin, where the pincers of the Soviet 5th Shock Army advancing from its bridgehead in the north and the 8th Guards Army coming up from its foothold in the south finally closed the circle around the city on 22nd March. The line of the German supply road through the Schlauch-Stellung (pipeline position) is indicated. This narrow corridor constituted a vital line of communication into and out of the fortress throughout most of the siege. (Brigham Young University)

Guards Army in the south was ordered to use two reinforced divisions of the 4th Guards Rifle Corps – the 47th and 57th Guards Rifle Divisions – for a main assault in two directions, north-west past Gorgast and west to Alt Tucheband. The 35th Guards Rifle Division was to make another secondary thrust to link up with the 416th Division coming down from the north. The operation was to begin on 22nd March.

On the night of 19th/20th March, the 25. Panzergrenadier-Division was relieved by Panzer-Division 'Müncheberg' (Generalmajor Werner Murmert), a new formation raised from the remnants of Panzerbrigade 103, which now became responsible for keeping open the Schlauch-Stellung.

Two days later, on 22nd March, after a whole night of air attacks and a massive artillery barrage, the Soviet attack on the corridor begun. Dorofeev's 295th Rifle Division, supported by around forty T-34 tanks from the 220th Tank Brigade, twenty-one ISU-152 self-propelled guns from the 396th Guards Heavy SP Gun Regiment and seventeen IS-2 tanks from the 89th Guards Heavy Tank Regiment, attacked from the north. German resistance was stiff and the Soviets only managed to get as close as half a kilometre from the vital Genschmar to Gorgast road.

South of the corridor, Shugayev's 47th Guards Rifle Division attacked and captured Gorgast as well as the nearby fort. Shortly after, the two Soviet pincers met at the Försterei Bridge over the Alte Oder stream north of Gorgast, thus uniting the two Soviet bridgeheads and finally completing the encirclement of Küstrin. The vital supply pipeline to the Festung was broken.

However, the ground gained by the Soviets had only been taken at considerable cost. The 9. Armee claimed 116 Soviet tanks destroyed during the day, the I. Abteilung of Panzer-Regiment 'Müncheberg', equipped with a company each of Panthers, PzKpfw IVs and Tigers, alone claiming 59 of them.

Over the following days, the Germans saw their bridgehead west of the Oder continue to shrink. All attempts by Panzer-Division 'Müncheberg' and the 25. Panzergrenadier-Division, released from 9. Armee reserve, to unblock the fortress proved futile due to the superior Soviet artillery and the inept way in which the German attacks were led. By now the Soviets had carved out a bridgehead of 300 square kilometres and they went over to the defence. The next few days brought further losses for the Germans, Mikhailovich's 416th Rifle Division captured the Alt Bleyen manor farm, which had been defended since the 19th by Füsilier-Bataillon 303. This was where the vital road from Gorgast connected with the Küstrin fortress, and the nearby village of Neu Bleyen.

On 27th March, the Germans made their last attempt to break through the Soviet lines and relieve the besieged fortress. Despite the fact that they had assembled a considerable force for this undertaking – the 25. Panzergrenadier-Division, the 20. Panzergrenadier-Division, the Führer-Grenadier-Division, the Panzer-Division 'Müncheberg', Kampfgruppe '1001 Nacht' (equipped with 49 Hetzers) and schwere SS-Panzer-Abteilung 502 (with Tiger IIs) – the attack was a complete failure. After an initial advance, all German formations were driven back to their starting points. The catastrophe was blamed on the enemy minefields; overwhelming artillery, rocket, mortar and anti-tank fire; well-constructed strong points in individual farmsteads; and the lack of cover in the completely flat and open country. German losses were very high, amounting to 1,292 men killed, wounded and missing. Thus, the fate of Küstrin was sealed.

ENDGAME

By mid-March the area controlled by the Germans had shrunk to the Altstadt peninsula, the Oder Island and a narrow strip on the west bank of the Vorflut-Kanal. Completely surrounded, the whole position was under continuous Soviet fire. The defenders were left with less than half of their original infantry force and hardly any heavy weapons or ammunition. Nonetheless, the German garrison was still a thorn in the side of the Soviets as it blocked the only westward railway line in the area and prevented access to a convenient site for bridge-building across the Oder. The following days brought even stronger Soviet shelling, including fire from captured German artillery pieces. The Soviet Air Force was visibly stronger, launching numerous air strikes on the fortress.

German riflemen passing the Pfarrkirche Sankt Marien (St Mary Parish Church) on Schlossfreiheit, the square in front of the castle. Note the broken windows and other damage from Soviet shelling. As the siege progressed, the church's crypt was used to shelter wounded. On the evening of 20th March Soviet artillery set the roof on fire, causing the nave and bell tower to collapse, burying everything under them including the wounded.
(BA Bild 146-1981-093-04)

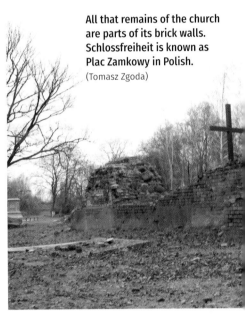

All that remains of the church are parts of its brick walls. Schlossfreiheit is known as Plac Zamkowy in Polish.
(Tomasz Zgoda)

On the evening of 20th March, the roof of the Sankt-Marien-Kirche church in the Altstadt collapsed after it was hit by artillery, burying an unknown number of wounded soldiers under the debris. The same fate befell those sheltered in the Rathaus (Town Hall) cellars. Those in other basements and casemates suffered due to the lack of medical supplies. Firemen tried in vain to put out the fires but all they could do was to blow up some of the buildings as a fire-brake to stop the flames from spreading. This saved the city's castle.

On 25th March, Marshal Zhukov ordered Chuikov's 8th Guards Army to capture what remained of the Festung. Chuikov planned a concentric attack with three divisions. The 82nd Guards Rifle Division (Major Georgy Khetagurov) was to strike from the south and capture the Altstadt via the land access route. Leading the attack would be the 242nd Guards Rifle Regiment with the 240th Guards Rifle Regiment following behind, each of them organised into company-size storm groups supported by IS-2 tanks, ISU-152 assault guns, 45mm and 76mm guns, 120mm mortars and captured Panzerfausts. Three batteries of 203mm heavy howitzers were

On 28th March, the Soviets started their final offensive against the Festung, launching three divisions in a concentric attack, and two days later Küstrin had fallen. Here, an ISU-152 self-propelled gun stands in front of the Berliner Tor, the city gate on the western side of the Altstadt. Note the Prussian eagle on top of the gate.
(Mahn- Und Gedenkstätte Seelower Höhen)

The gate, known in Polish as Brama Berlinska, has been neatly restored but without the eagle which was expurgated by the Soviets between September and October 1945. (Tomasz Zgoda)

positioned around the surrounded enclave to provide direct fire on the brick fortifications. The 416th Rifle Division (from the 5th Shock Army) was to make an additional assault on the Altstadt peninsula from the east, crossing over from the Neustadt.

The 35th Guards Rifle Division was to assault from the west. Its 100th Guards Rifle Regiment was to break the German resistance on the Vorflut-Kanal, then cross the canal and capture the Oder Island. The 101st Guards Rifle Regiment was to provide covering fire during the crossing and later itself cross over to northern part of the island. The division's third regiment, the 102nd, was to stay west of the canal and secure the Kietz suburb.

On 27th March, the Soviets sent an envoy to the German command with a call to surrender. No reply was received. That same day the Bienenhof, the strong point on the southern approach to the Altstadt defended so doggedly for two months, finally fell to the 82nd Guards Rifle Division, and shortly after so did the Kietzerbusch railway station just south of the Altstadt. There followed some ferocious close-quarter fighting in the restricted area in front of the Kietzer Tor (Kietz Gate) in which the railway station changed hands several times.

The following day the Soviets unleashed their massed assault. At dawn, elements of Mikhailovich's 416th Rifle Division crossed the Warthe and captured the area north of the Altstadt. Shortly after, the three heavy howitzer batteries began methodically blasting the Altstadt fortifications. To add to their woes Soviet ground-attack aircraft began bombing and strafing the defenders. Next came a forty-minute barrage on the German positions and following that the main attacks began. In the south, Khetagurov's 82nd Guards Rifle Division moved forward and by noon had finally and decisively captured the Kietzerbusch station. In the west, Zaiolyev's 35th Guards Rifle Division crossed the Vorflut-Kanal, the crossing site covered by a smoke-screen and its assault boats reaching the Oder Island after just six minutes. However, their advance was stopped in front of Lunette B, an old fort to the south of the Artillery Barracks.

The fighting for the approaches to the Altstadt was so fierce that it was late afternoon before the attackers reached the market square and the castle area. A hastily organised German counter-attack managed to stop the Soviets but only for a while.

The situation in the Altstadt was now so calamitous that Reinefarth ordered the withdrawal of all forces to the Oder Island. The order was to be carried out under cover of darkness. To stop a further Soviet advance, the only remaining bridge linking the Altstadt with the Oder Island, the railway bridge, had to be blown shortly after 2100-hrs, even though numerous soldiers were still manning it. Several other troops and a considerable number of Volkssturm were consequently cut-off in the Altstadt. A few managed to cross in the remaining inflatable boats and fishing vessels but the river was too swollen for anyone to attempt swimming across.

That night Reinefarth radioed the 9. Armee for permission to break out

Soviet soldiers survey the devastation on the Marktplatz square in the centre of the Altstadt, the scene of heavy combat before the final surrender of the last defenders. The Kriegerdenkmal (warriors memorial), erected to commemorate the citizens of Küstrin that fell during the Franco-Prussian War of 1870-71, has survived the onslaught relatively intact. The ruins in the background are all that remains of the Rathaus (town hall). Note the M3 half-track in the left background, another American-produced vehicle nearly a thousand of which (in various variants) were delivered to the Soviet Union under Lend-Lease. (Timofej Melni

Memories of former battles fade and today all that is left of the memorial are its foundations. So little is left of the Altstadt that today in Poland it is called 'Küstrin's Pompeii'.
(Tomasz Zgoda)

Soviet M3 half-tracks towing anti-tank guns move across the Oder over a wooden trestle bridge erected by Red Army engineers. They are crossing over from the Oder Island to the Altstadt. In the background lie the wrecked road and railway bridges. This picture was taken by official Red Army combat photographer Timofej Melnik.
(Deutsch- Russisches Museum Berlin-Karlshorst KH203296)

Looking north-west across the Oder from Poland into Germany. The two bridges have been resurrected. (Tomasz Zgoda)

with his garrison. Busse's headquarters tried to obtain Hitler's approval but the Führer, enraged by the failure of the force to hold the position, refused any evacuation. Instead, he demanded that Reinefarth be arrested and court-martialled.

Throughout the 29th, the remnants of the battered garrison were confined to the Oder Island. The 35th Guards Rifle Division stormed the Artillery Barracks but the Germans held their ground. However, their attempts to recapture Lunette B proved futile. In the meantime, additional Soviet troops crossed over from the northern end of the Altstadt peninsula and captured the island's railway station. Throughout the day there was hand-to-hand fighting, which left both sides exhausted and the Germans out of ammunition.

That evening, notwithstanding Hitler's orders, Reinefarth decided to abandon the Oder Island on his own initiative. His plan was that those troops

Lieutenant-General Nikolai Berzarin (in front), commander of the 5th Shock Army, and a party of his subordinate officers leave after inspecting the Neues Werk fort in the Neustadt, the site of the Germans' last stand in that part of the city. Built in 1863-72, during the siege it was held by elements of Kampgruppe Krüger, and it was the 3rd Battalion of the 1038th Rifle Regiment of the 295th Rifle Division of the 32nd Rifle Corps from Berzarin's army that, after a massive artillery bombardment, finally captured the fort on 12th March.

The fort was demolished after the war. Nowadays only a cobbled street, parts of the fort's embankment and a brick wall are all that remain along Ulica Sportowa.
(Tomasz Zgoda)

that could would attack westwards in the hope that at least some of his men would be able to reach friendly lines. The intention was to break out in two directions. Soldiers from Kampfgruppe Schulz, Füsilier-Bataillon 303 and a contingent from Panzer-Division 'Müncheberg' were directed through the Soviet lines near Kuhbrücken-Vorstadt and from there were to advance south of Alt Bleyen aiming to reach the German lines north of Golzow, a distance of nearly eight kilometres. The second group took another route and went south-west. Both forces eventually split up into individuals and small parties wandering through the darkness in unknown terrain. Beyond the three lines of Soviet trenches facing Küstrin, they came across the burnt-out hulks of tanks destroyed in the earlier fighting, battled their way through another three lines of westward-facing Soviet trenches, and eventually reached friendly lines at dawn. As they approached, they were accidentally hit by a German artillery barrage, which caused numerous casualties. Some 1,000-1,300 men are said to have got through, including Reinefarth, NSDAP Kreisleiter Körner and 118 Volkssturm.

By then the fighting in the Altstadt had reached its end too. Early on the morning of the 29th, after a last conference in a bunker, in which unit commanders were given permission to try and break out with their men, the commander of Volkssturm-Bataillon 16/186, Hauptmann Rudolf Tamm, negotiated a surrender with the Soviets. A few isolated parties fought on, only to be executed on the spot after capture. The last fighting died out on 30th March.

After holding out for two months, Festung Küstrin had finally fallen. The Soviet high command could not announce that they had taken it for a second time so instead they claimed destruction of 'a strong German garrison west and south-west of Küstrin defending an area between the Warthe and the Oder'.

DIE ARBRECHNUNG

Two months of combat had turned Küstrin into a pile of rubble. Ninety per cent of the Neustadt had been destroyed, as had the entire Altstadt. The castle and all churches lay in ruins, and all of the city's bridges had been destroyed. Only the old fortifications survived.

The fighting had been costly on both sides. In the Neustadt around 3,500 Germans had been killed or wounded, and roughly the same number had been taken prisoner. Out of around 2,700 men who remained in the Altstadt and Kietz, some 1,400-1,700 had fallen or been captured during the last three weeks of fighting.

Soviet losses were even higher. The 32nd Rifle Corps lost 2,229 men killed, 7,730 wounded and at least 299 men due to other causes. Of the 8th Guards Army's formations that completed the reduction of the Altstadt, the 82nd Guards Rifle Division had 85 men killed and 379 wounded. Incomplete figures for the 35th Guards Rifle Division show at least 431 killed and 700

A Red Army female traffic regulator, A. Batyanova, giving directions on the Stern crossroads in the Neustadt after the battle. She is standing at the beginning of Borndorfer Strasse, the thoroughfare leading out of the city to the north, and the traffic signs on the left point (top to bottom) to Berlin, Frankfurt-an-der-Oder, Poznan (Posen), Neudamm (nowadays Debno in Poland) and a Crossing for Light Vehicles.

As in many other places in present-day Kostrzyn nad Odra (the Polish name for Küstrin on the Oder, but actually only encompassing what used to be the Neustadt), all pre-war buildings around the crossroads have been demolished and replaced by modern development.
(Tomasz Zgoda)

wounded in February and March. The 47th Guards Rifle Division probably had similar losses. Supporting armoured, artillery and engineer units had suffered high losses in men and equipment.

The actions described in this book represent no more than highlights of the similar struggle that was taking place along the length of the eastern front as the Soviet Winter Offensive played out its course.

THE BEGINNING OF THE END

The Soviet Spring offensive had swept across Poland more quickly than either side would have imagined. The retreating German army was overwhelmed and in confusion, overmatched and outpaced by the Soviets. That any resistance could be cobbled together was surprising and, under the circumstances, the length of time the final outposts managed to hold off the Soviet onslaught remains remarkable. In mitigation, the Red Army had overrun its supply capability and maintaining a fast-paced offensive had an extremely detrimental effect on men and materiel. Also, the nature of the fighting, with terrain often best suited to defence, served to prolong the agony.

Posen fell on 23rd February, Schwedt on 27th February, Zehden held out until 27th March. Küstrin's collapse on 30th March marked the end of Germany's final outpost east of the Oder. With its fall, the stage was set for the First Byelorussian Front's final offensive. On 16th April, the Soviet army crossed the Oder in massive force and began the final offensive that would lead to Berlin and the end of the Third Reich.

The fighting in the early months of 1945 play out as a human tragedy. One side desperately defending their homeland against an invader, fighting to the bitter end, with what few resources they could muster, in order to save their homes and families. The other side driven to end a war which had been inflicted on it, determined to see the conflict through to its completion, no matter the cost. For both sides the end was so clearly in sight. The resolve to risk everything for your cause and sacrifice all must have been an intolerable hurdle to climb when there was a tangible chance the combatants could survive to enjoy the peace.

Organisation Tables

Soviet Tank Corps 1944 - 1945

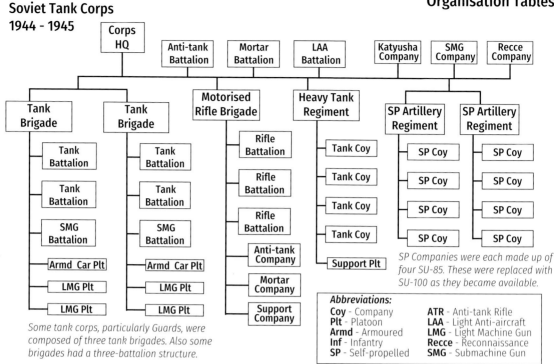

Some tank corps, particularly Guards, were composed of three tank brigades. Also some brigades had a three-battalion structure.

SP Companies were each made up of four SU-85. These were replaced with SU-100 as they became available.

Abbreviations:
- **Coy** - Company
- **Plt** - Platoon
- **Armd** - Armoured
- **Inf** - Infantry
- **SP** - Self-propelled
- **ATR** - Anti-tank Rifle
- **LAA** - Light Anti-aircraft
- **LMG** - Light Machine Gun
- **Recce** - Reconnaissance
- **SMG** - Submachine Gun

When compared to the equivalent composition of the units of other nations, the Soviet model can be confusing. The tank 'corps' shown above was the equivalent of the German panzer division. Similarly, the subordinate units largely equate to smaller units in other armies. Tank battalions were composed of only 21 tanks - by this time usually the T-34/85. The five tank 'companies' of the heavy tank 'regiment' would represent a troop or platoon in other Allied structures. As noted above, there was a degree of fluidity in the precise organisation, often based on the political patronage of the formation, the more favoured formations having 'Guards' status. Taken as a whole, with its mix of medium and heavy tanks, plus the potent assault guns of the self-propelled artillery units, the Soviet tank corps was a formidable organisation in 1945 and could comprise up to 200 armoured fighting vehicles, compared to 160 to 180 in a full strength panzer division.

Soviet Infantry Division 1943 - 1945

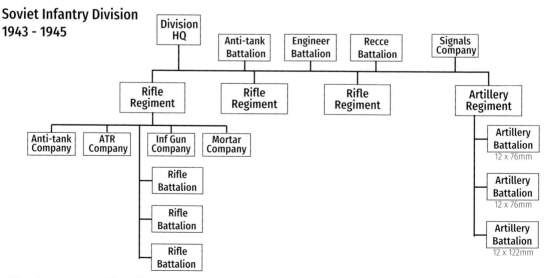

After the catastrophic defeats of 1941, the Soviet Army hollowed out the divisional structure so that it had the bare minimum of support units. Thereafter, most support arms, especially artillery, was held in dedicated specialised formations intended to act en-mass.

anzer Division — 1944

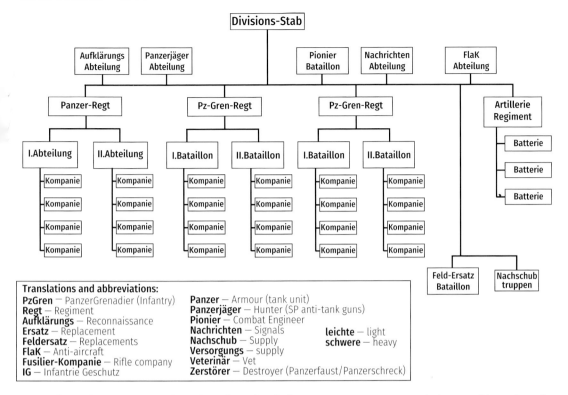

By the time of the collapse of the front in Poland, the German Army was rarely in a position where it could field entire and complete divisions. Divisions shown within the order-of-battle were most often deployed as Kampfgruppen — battlegroups — utilising whichever units were available and useful for the task in hand.

Volksgrenadier Division — 1944

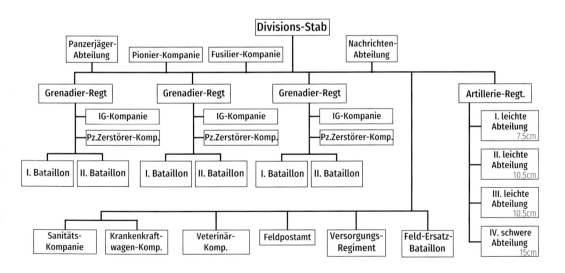

Glossary

Abschnitt – Unit or section.
Abteilung – The equivalent of a battalion for certain units, like armour and artillery. Also used as a more generic term similar in use to 'unit'.
Alarm-Einheite – 'Emergency unit', a body of troops brought together on an ad-hoc basis.
Ausbildungs – Training or instruction.
Bataillon – Battalion.
Bürgermeister – Town mayor.
Ersatz – Substitute or replacement.
Fahnenjunker – Officer Training.
Fallschirmjager – German Paratrooper. Regarded as an elite force and recruited by the Luftwaffe.
Festungen – Fortresses, bunkers and other defensive structures.
FlaK **Fliegerabwehrkanone** – Literally 'aircraft-defence gun', or more commonly anti-aircraft gun.
Gauleiter – Senior district leader within the Nazi Party structure.
Geschütz – Artillery gun.
Heeresgruppe – Army group.
IG **Infantriegeschütz** – Infantry Support Gun
Jagdverband – Literally 'hunting group'.
Kampfgruppe – Battlegroup – and ad-hoc grouping of sub-units created for a specific task or battle.
Kriegsberichter – German war photographer.
Landeschütz – German units composed of overage reservists.
lFH **leichte Feldhaubitze** – Light field howitzer.
Katyusha – Russian mobile multiple rocket system.
NSDAP-Ortsgruppenleiter – Nazi Party local group leader.
OKH **Oberkommando des Heeres** — Supreme Command of the German Army.
OT **Organisation Todt** – The specialist civil engineering service created by Dr Fritz Todt.
PaK **Panzerabwehrkanone** – Anti-tank gun.
Panzerfaust – 'Tank fist' – hand-held single use anti-tank weapon.
Panzerjäger-Abteilung – Tank hunter battalion.
Panzerschreck – Hand-held anti-tank weapon, similar to the 'bazooka'.
Panzerturm – Armoured turret.
Pioniere – German term for military engineers.
Ravelin – Detached outer defences of a Vauban style fortification.
Redoubt – A bastion or central fortification.
sFH **schwere Feldhaubitze** – Heavy field howitzer.
Scharfschützen – Sniper
Stäbe – Command staff of German military units.
Stadtkommandant – Town commander.
Stellung – Position.
Stevedores – Dock workers employed loading and unloading ships (derived from Spanish/Portugueses).
StuG **Sturmgeschütz** – Self propelled assault gun.
Sturmgewehr – Infantry assault rifle
StuH **Sturmhaubitze** – Self-propelled assault howitzer.
Volksgrenadier – Literally 'People's Soldier', a late-war reorganisation of some Wehrmacht units.
Volkssturm – German Home Guard militia.
Wehrkreise – Army District.
Wellenbrecher – 'Breakwater', used in the sense of a barrier for an oncoming enemy offensive.
Wehrmacht – the German Army from 16th March 1935.
Zug – Group or section.